AIDS and You

To Sheila, my best friend, closest advisor and source of endless encouragement for over 30 years., and to all who have been part of the ACET family over the years.

And with grateful thanks to Ray & Joy Thomas for insisting that a new edition be written, to Mark Forshaw for writing a new chapter on projects, to George Verwer for helping make it all happen, to Susie Howe for helping get copies quickly around the world, to Tear Fund for allowing adaption of their AIDS manual and to friends at CANA and EHA for many helpful comments and suggestions for this India edition.

Dr Patrick Dixon

AIDS and You

Dr Patrick Dixon

Jointly published by
Operation Mobilisation
&
ACET International Alliance
in partnership with Kingsway

Aids and You
Copyright © 2002, by Dr. Patrick Dixon

Revised 3rd Edition, 2002
Reprint 2003
Revised 4th edtion 2004
Three reprints 2005-2007
Reprint 2008
ISBN: 978-81-7362-470-4

Any part of this book may be reproduced for educational and training purposes with full acknowledgement and reference to the ACET International website: http:// www.acet-international.org where the full book text may be found.

Third Edtion co-sponsored and published by Operation Mobilisation and the ACET International Alliance in partnership with Kingsway.

All royalties from the sale of this book have been set aside to help copies reach those who need them.

First edtion published by Kingsway 1989 as AIDS and Young People, reprinted 1990, Editions in Thai, Portugese, Czech, Romanian, Hungarian, Spanish, Russian, Turkish, Urdu, Baite, German, French and Polish.

Jointly published by
Operation Mobilisation
and
ACET International Alliance
in partnership with Kingsway

Printed in India by
Authentic India, Secunderabad 500003
email: printing@ombooks.org

About the Author

Patrick Dixon is author of 12 books including *The Truth about AIDS, AIDS and You, Out of the Ghetto and into the City, Signs of Revival, The Truth about Drugs, The Genetic Revolution, The Truth about Westminster, The Rising Price of Love* and *Futurewise.*

He trained as a doctor before specialising in the care of those dying of cancer and then of AIDS. Following the launch of The Truth about AIDS he started ACET (AIDS Care Education and Training) in June 1988, as a national and international Christian response to AIDS. Dr Dixon was CEO until 1991 and today helps lead an international network of independent initiatives known as the ACET International Alliance.

Dr Dixon is Chairman of Global Change Ltd, a consulting and trends forecasting company, a frequent commentator in media around the world and an adviser to many large corporations on issues such as the digital society, new technology, biotech, globalisation, leadership, motivation and corporate values. He is 45 years old, lives in West London and is married with four children. As a family they are active members of a local church, in partnership with the Evangelical Alliance and Pioneer.

More Copies of this book:
More copies of this book may be ordered free by Christian Organisations for distribution in developing countries.
email :   isdixon@dircon.co.uk
      or
            cana@vsnl.com

Contents

Contents

Introduction

An Urgent Response to AIDS

Unless something changes over 20 crore men, women and children will die because of AIDS. Already more than 50 crore people know a friend or relative who has died – just one of the 4 crore adults and children with AIDS, buried or cremated by the start of 2002. Yet despite all that, this new epidemic is spreading faster than ever among the poorest nations, killing four times as many people every year as a decade ago. People just don't realise the danger — or don't want to think about it.

I will never forget the first person I met myself with AIDS: a young student desperately ill in a hospital side-room. He was anxious, restless, sweaty, fighting for every breath, suffocating in his own secretions and gripped with terrible fear. He had a gas mask over his face and tubes running into his body. He was totally alone in that awful room and about to die.

I was so shocked that anyone in a London teaching hospital, with all the facilities in the world, should be abandoned in such a state. But that's how things were back in 1987, a time when no hospice in Britain would accept someone with AIDS, when some nurses refused to visit people with AIDS at home and when some of my fellow doctors refused to prescribe appropriate medicines.

Just because these people had the wrong diagnosis:

AIDS

From that moment on I was involved. Here on that ward was a human being made in God's image, in great need. How could I respond other than to care and help, laying aside any personal feelings I might have had about lifestyles, and the means by which he had become infected?

His family didn't even know he was ill (he was afraid they would reject him and wanted to take his secret to the grave) and the medicines he was getting were doing nothing to relieve his suffering. It was as if 20 years of hospice medicine had been thrown out of the window.

I was trained as a cancer doctor, looking after those close to death at home. For several years I had kept my distance from AIDS – someone else's speciality and not an illness I was naturally drawn to, in fact the opposite — but when I saw for myself the ghastly reality, the stigma, the shocking rejection of sick people by fellow professionals, and all on my own doorstep, I realised that the skills some of us had in care of those dying of cancer needed to be extended urgently to those with AIDS as well.

But it wasn't just care workers that were rejecting people with AIDS: the church was also caught up with finger pointing and moral debates, and taking very little practical action. I had been just as bad in some ways, finding every excuse in the book not to get involved with this strange new illness. And then I realised how heartless I had been, and how my attitude had to change radically.

That young man died peacefully, several days later, with the right treatment, and with his loving family by his side, but the whole episode shook me profoundly. I would never be the same again.

This book was originally published in 1989, as a shorter version of The Truth about AIDS, to encourage a practical compassionate response to AIDS by churches of every denomination, focussed on community care and schools prevention. It has been revised and updated once more at the request of people from all over the world, who have asked for a short "action" book about AIDS from a Christian perspective, and with strong encouragement from Ray and Joy Thomas (AIDS Intercessors), George Verwer (Operation Mobilisation) and Mark Forshaw (Africa Inland Mission).

Almost everything I warned about in 1989 is sadly today a reality, yet in all the great suffering and grief of many millions of people there is still hope that the future may not be a repeat of the past. What is very upsetting is that so many of the lessons of the African epidemic back in the late 1980s have not yet been learned in other parts of the world fifteen years later. Even now we still see denial by governments and entire nations who seem to think that somehow "it will never happen to us. We will only have a few cases". And still the prejudice and fear remains in many places.

With over 8 crore already HIV infected the epidemic is still in the earliest stages. Mumbai alone is seeing over 1,000 new infections every night and India could see more HIV cases over the next 15 years than there have been in the entire world until now. African-style spread (across Asia) is beginning to take place in many other countries. History is now repeating itself, on a vast and tragic scale, yet with worryingly few signs of the kind of aggressive multi-level government responses we saw in places like Uganda 15 years ago.

Christians are now leading the fight against AIDS in many nations. In South Africa, Archbishop Desmond Tutu estimates churches and Christian organisations are providing over 60% of HIV community programmes in Africa. In India the Christian response to AIDS has already mobilised well over 25,000 workers, part-time or full time,

11

all of whom are involved in care or prevention. This is a remarkable achievement, a people-movement across the nation. We know this through the Christian AIDS National Alliance (CANA) in Delhi, a growing network of several hundred Christian agencies.

We also see it in the ACET International Alliance, a global community of independent agencies, some grown from small beginnings back in 1988, all seeking to make a compassionate response in the name of Christ. We see it in hundreds of missionary and development organisations like Operation Mobilisation, Samaritan's Purse, Tear Fund, World Vision, Christian AID and the Salvation Army.

Uganda is a wonderful example of what can happen when governments and Faith-Based Organisations (FBOs) work in partnership. The AIDS Control Programme has seen a dramatic fall in infection rates, particularly among the young — from 22% to less than 8%. This could not have been achieved without church support. It's a sign of hope for the future.

Christians from every tradition can unite easily in two simple aims:

◆ Unconditional, compassionate care for all affected by HIV / AIDS
◆ Effective prevention respecting and upholding the historic teachings of the church

So often as Christians reacting to AIDS we do nothing or rush to open our bibles, or the teachings of the church, to declare that something is wrong. Yet in our response we can lose sight of God's mercy, love and forgiveness — and the reality that many are infected through actions of others rather than their own behaviour. It is possible to be technically correct in interpreting God's standards yet terribly wrong in our own attitudes.

Take the example of Jesus with the woman caught in adultery recounted in John's Gospel — really the story of the missing man. Here are a bunch of angry men, looking for an excuse to lynch a woman, yet two people sinned and the man is nowhere to be seen. In Jesus' day there was a hierarchy: woman sex sin punished by death, other sin was more or less acceptable, while man sex sin was hardly worth fussing about.

Jesus loathed their double standards.

He cut right through them with just one sentence: "If any one of you is without sin let him be the first to throw a stone". "Yes you sir, whose eyes have never strayed the section of the magazine stall which stores pornography material, you who have never been jealous, spiteful, rude or have never gossiped behind someone's back, you who are the perfect wife, you who have never lost your temper with the children, you who have never told a half-truth or broken the speed limit. Come and cast the stone." (see John 8:1-11)

No one moved. Jesus stared them all out until they all left one by one — the oldest first. In one sentence Jesus totally destroyed any possibility of judging others according to a ranking of sin. All of us have sinned and fallen short of God's glory, all are utterly dead outside of God's grace.

When it comes to pointing the finger, Jesus forbids us to put ourselves on a pedestal. He was the only person on this earth who had the right to condemn yet he says to the woman "neither do I condemn you". He also adds "go now and leave your life of sin".

As Christians we get confused between the two things Jesus said: either we rush to make moral statements, tripping up over judgmental attitudes along the way, or we rush to express God's mercy and love, falling into a deep hole where there is no longer a clear moral framework. The Jesus way is to hold infinite love and perfect standards in tension together — something we need his help to do.

Let us be absolutely clear that the teaching of scripture from Genesis to Revelation is constant regarding the wonderful gift of sex union, as a celebration of love and friendship between a man and woman committed together for life. God saw that all He created was good including sex, it's the waste of sex outside marriage that causes him grief. The bible makes clear that all sex union outside marriage is wrong. This has always been the teaching of the church — in common with the Jewish faith and Islam.

Sex is shown to be a mystery, a spiritual event when two become "one flesh". We see the physical side of this whenever a sperm fuses with an egg. Half a cell from a woman fuses with half a cell from a man to form literally one flesh: a new unique individual full of future personality and identity.

So how do we live with these tensions? The way of Jesus is clear: we are called to express the unconditional love of God to all in need regardless of how they come to be so.

If someone is seriously hurt in a car crash just outside my house I rush out to help. I don't walk away just because I find out he's drunk and that is why there was an accident. Nor do I start preaching anti-drunkenness sermons in the ambulance or on the ward. I do however talk about the story wherever I go, pointing out dangers of drinking and driving.

With those affected by HIV/AIDS we are called to be helpful, to care and express love.

We are there as servants to help as the person wishes and it is a privilege to do so. Many are shocked to find Christians involved who care deeply while unable to endorse certain lifestyles.

I often think about the story Jesus told of the prodigal son who took his inheritance and went to spend it on himself many miles from home. What would have happened if he had become infected with HIV while away and had died before having had time to think again? I imagine his father reading the newspaper over breakfast one day and seeing the death notice of his own son. I imagine him breaking down in tears as he calls his wife: "He never phoned, he never wrote, and in ten years we had no news except through friends of friends".

Many people with AIDS today are dying without hope and without God. I think of our heavenly Father, tears pouring down his face, not wanting any to perish, nor to be separated one day more, yet with sadness releasing people to go their own way.

Those with AIDS today are just like the lepers of Jesus' time facing fear and rejection. When Jesus touched the leper he made history — still talked about 2000 years later. It was the most powerful demonstration of the love of God that he could possibly have shown other than his own sacrificial death.

When a church volunteer goes into a home that person carries the presence of Christ. Jesus has no body of his own: the church is his body. We are his hands, his feet, his smile, his voice, his heart, his touch.

The only part of God that people see could be the life of Jesus in you or me. As we go into the home, and give someone a hug or take someone's hand, and bring water or medicines or food, we too are making a bit of history: a powerful declaration of God's love, a prophetic statement of his heart to people who often feel totally alienated from the church.

There is also a time for explaining God's design for living. Faced with a world disaster resulting largely from ignoring God's ways it would be unimaginable for the church to be silent. It is a fact that if everyone kept to one partner for life, and ceased injecting drugs, HIV would be wiped off the face of this earth in less than 30 years. It is also true that continuing without restraint over the same period could cost over 20 crore people's lives.

As we will see, condoms reduce risk but are no answer for the long term. Are governments honestly expecting a couple where one or other may have HIV to go on using condoms for 50 years "just in case"? What happens when they want to have children or when it breaks, leaks, falls off or fails in some other way? Pregnancy rates are high with condoms. The pill produced the "revolution" in the 1960s not the condom. Condoms are also a very expensive option for countries like India with millions of the poorest people, and tiny budgets — only Rs.100 per person a year to spend on health. We have to find more sustainable, culturally appropriate solutions for the 200 crore people who earn less than Rs.100 a day.

That's why The World Health Organisation declared: "the most effective way to prevent transmission of HIV is to abstain, or for two uninfected individuals to be faithful to one another. Alternatively the correct use of a condom may reduce the risk significantly". (World AIDS Day 1990)

The only way for many partners to be sure of safety may be HIV tests. In some countries up to a third of women with AIDS have been celibate and then monogamous, yet are dying because their husbands were infected through other relationships. This is a controversial and sensitive area. Anyone considering a test needs expert advice first.

How to help:

Compassionate care for the ill and dying, saving lives through prevention, and community development go hand in hand. Those involved in care often have the greatest credibility and impact. Then people can see the reality of the illness, change behaviour and be motivated to help the dying and orphans left behind. But changing behaviour can be hard when someone is destitute and takes risks every day selling her body to survive. Poverty, poor education and AIDS go hand in hand. The poorer people are, the faster AIDS usually spreads.

Is your church or organisation prepared at leadership level for AIDS ? Any growing church may find people with HIV as members as a result of previous lifestyles.

People with AIDS can be very sensitive to reactions: will this new person accept or reject? As with cancer a person can swing rapidly from anger, to denial, sadness, despair, hope, optimism, questioning, resignation, fighting, giving up, wanting active treatment, or even wanting to die.

Be sensitive to where the person is today, helping the person understand that in the midst of great uncertainties about the future, your own constant support and friendship is not in doubt, just as God's faithfulness and love is not in doubt.

There may be deep wounds from the past, and feelings of worthlessness. Guilt over unintentional passing of infection on to others, guilt over surviving when so many others have already died, and guilt about lifestyles may all be present. Feelings of isolation and loneliness may be intense. Fear of the process of dying is often far greater than the fear of death itself.

The greatest need is often for simple practical help rather than just for comforting words or a listening ear. Cleaning up a person or cooking food can say more about your care for the person and their children than six hours of sitting in a comfortable chair. Many want to counsel someone with AIDS — but who is really prepared to go the extra mile?

And when life is over, the children remain. Ten million have been orphaned already. Who looks after them? And who is fighting to save the lives of the next generation of young parents, warning them every day about the risks of AIDS?

These things are what this book is about.

Yet while HIV infection spreads ever faster, so does the Christian faith with more people becoming followers of Christ around the world over the last twenty years than has ever happened in such a small time before, especially in the poorest nations. My prayer is that this spread of life-changing faith will help prevent the spread of HIV, and will provoke new compassion, care and understanding.

Patrick Dixon
October 2002

Chapter One

AIDS Is Your Problem Too

Within a few years every person in the world will probably know personally someone who has died because of AIDS. More than one in 200 of all adults walking on the earth are infected already. It may be an older brother or sister, a cousin, an uncle, a friend, a man in the same street, a shopkeeper, or someone at school or at work. It's already the case in most of Africa and parts of South East Asia. You may not realise it because AIDS is kept so secret. You may think the person died of cancer, or something else, but someone somewhere knows otherwise.

By 2002 over 8 crore people had probably been infected with HIV — no one knows accurate figures. And HIV is spreading twice as fast across the world today as five years ago.

Some people freak out. They turn the TV channels over whenever AIDS is mentioned. They get scared, if they think someone at the function last night had the disease.

They panic about the thought of touching someone with AIDS or picking up a dirty glass without realising and drinking from it. If they actually think several people may have been infected, then panic turns to hysteria.

Ambulance men in "space-suits"

In the early days of the epidemic people acted in strange ways. In the UK, police turned up wearing gloves, masks and overshoes to arrest a suspect, in case he was infected. Ambulance men turned up to transport someone who could have AIDS wearing 'space-suits'. A priest offered someone Holy Communion wearing gloves, with a bit of bread stuck on the edge of a wooden spatula. Old ladies in churches went back to their seats without drinking the wine. Meals-on-wheels delivery service of a hot meal to the home of someone who was ill became a stone–cold meal left on the doorstep because the driver was too scared to ring the bell and go inside.

In Calcutta, India, a brand new AIDS ward was padlocked shut because no doctors or nurses could be found to work in it. In the same city a mother and newborn baby were thrown onto the streets when the medics found the mother had HIV infection. In Uganda fellow villagers have turned their backs in the past on people with AIDS dying without food or water, in case they died themselves entering the homes of the sick.

Whatever the culture, whatever the nation, you will find examples of stigma, rejection, hostility and abuse to those with AIDS. Thankfully attitudes are changing in many places but the burden is still there. As a doctor I know of no other illness in living memory that has caused such widespread reactions. Why?

Fear soon turns to anger. Bricks fly through windows or the home is burnt to the ground (this has happened twice in London). People are sacked on the spot and thrown out of their homes. Children are thrown out of schools. It happened in India. And the problem keeps on growing.

Bored rigid with AIDS

Most people I meet in Western countries are bored rigid with AIDS until they meet someone who has it. It is a terrible shock to find your best friend is dying. It is even worse when you find that no one will talk about it because he has the wrong disease. He doesn't have cancer, and it is as if he has ceased to exist. No one wants to know.

But in countries like Rwanda, Burundi, Zimbabwe, South Africa or Uganda it's very different: every family has experienced AIDS grief and death is ever present — just look at the coffin makers by the side of the road or the steady trail of mourners at cemeteries in South Africa, where space is running out for burials in many cities because of AIDS. But where AIDS is so overwhelming there's another problem: people turn off, slipping into denial.

AIDS is the silent killer because by the time. you know you've got it it's too late. But the trouble is that HIV is spreading fast with 15,000 new infections every day, and in spite of what many Westerners have been told, most of the people infected worldwide are neither gay men nor drug addicts.

And despite what many in the poorest nations have been told, many people dying with HIV have been celibate before marriage and faithful as most married women of India are, but infected by partners or medical treatments with infected blood or dirty needles.

Many people in countries like India aren't worried about AIDS because no one they know is dying — yet. But the problem is that by the time you know one friend who is ill, you will probably know a hundred people who are infected and going to die in the future. There is a big time delay.

Chain reaction

People you see on the TV, or read about in the papers, may have been infected in the early 1990s. For the last five to ten years they have felt completely well, perhaps totally unaware of the situation and may have passed on the infection.

One year, only two people in a community are infected, but within twelve months the number has risen to four. By the time another year is up the number has risen to eight and a year later it reaches sixteen. Everyone is well and looking fit. No one has even the remotest idea that anything is wrong. After another year-and-a-half forty are doomed, and a year later almost 100. This kind of pattern of spread has been common in Africa and other parts of the world.

And then one of the people infected early on has a mysterious viral illness and is out of action for six weeks. When he returns he looks really tired, but within a week or two he is back in action again. Six months later his friends notice that he has lost some weight, and one night after dinner he is rushed off to the hospital because he can't breathe.

One of his mates turns up to see him the next day to find he has died of pneumonia. A week later his brother tells someone in the bar that the doctors suspect he died of AIDS. That same night the 102nd person in the club took a risk with someone he thought he knew was 'safe' and became infected. So if you know that ten people in your city or town have died of AIDS, you know that maybe between 250 and 1,000 are walking around the streets every day feeling fine but carrying the killer virus.

Spreading like wildfire

In every country of the world each person with HIV has often infected another person within a few months. If the people remain alive, then it means the numbers with HIV double quite fast.

The same thing happens with other viruses — like the one causing colds. On the first day of term one person has a cold. Over, the following weeks the numbers only rise slowly at first: one, then two, -then four, then eight, then sixteen, then thirty-two. After the fifth week of term something dramatic happens and sixty-four new people go down with a cold. The week after it is even worse and 128 are sniffing and sneezing. After another week 256 are feeling rotten and the week after that 512 want to have a day off.

The way the cold virus spreads shows you how HIV can spread — but with one or two important differences. With HIV the time for numbers infected to double is not a week but often starts off in a country at around six to twelve months. After thousands of people have been infected, the doubling time slows down, perhaps to a couple of years, as it would have done in the school.

Injecting death

It is true, however, that while the spread of HIV through sexual contact is relatively slow, because most people do not swop partners every day of every week, the spread from injecting drugs can be extremely fast, with one addict infecting at least one other person every day. Drug addicts can often share the same syringe for more doses. Each addict may inject themselves several times a day. In this situation the numbers of people infected could go over a period of weeks from one, to two, to four, to eight, to sixteen, to thirty-two, to sixty-four, to 128, to 256, to 512 to over 1,000. This is why Italy, New York, parts of Scotland and other places with a bad drugs problem such as Manipur in North East India soon had a terrible AIDS problem.

Could the whole world die?

AIDS is unlikely to wipe us all out. Within any group, town or nation it spreads rapidly through those most at risk, it spreads more slowly through those at medium risk and spreads very slowly through those at low risk. How many people are infected, and how quickly, depends quite simply on how many people there are in each of those groups. If we can persuade people to change from high-risk living to low-risk living, then we can at least slow down the spread. In Uganda the percentage of young women carrying HIV has fallen dramatically from around 22% to 7%. Education saves lives but it takes time to change the behaviour of an entire community.

Who is 'safe'?

In Italy they talk about AIDS as a plague of drug addicts. In Africa it is known as a plague of men and women. In the UK it was first labelled a plague affecting the gay community ... but all that is changing. AIDS is a disease of relationships and the virus causing it spreads along the lines of relationships. It spreads through a men's drinking club, a factory, an office, a youth club and a school.

One thing is sure: AIDS knows no boundaries of nation, colour, personality or sexual orientation. The virus crosses between sexes and between people of the same sex when they have sex together, or when blood or secretions from one person enter the blood-stream of another.

In the UK, as in the USA, the first group to be badly affected was the male homosexual community. As we have seen, one group only has to be hit a few years earlier than another to have a problem 100 times greater. That creates a misleading impression that you only really develop AIDS if you are a member of that group.

Heads in the sand

People always think they are safe until it is too late - and governments are no exception. In San Francisco they knew all about this strange new illness called AIDS that killed young men in New York and Los Angeles. They were worried and started to look for signs of spread into their own community. They missed it. By the time they realised they had a problem, one in four of the entire gay community was already infected. It's been the same story in many parts of Africa and in Asia regarding spread between men and women.

Many pastors have their heads in the sand. "We don't have a problem of AIDS in our church" they tell me. "In that case your church must be unique", I reply. Whenever a church is growing, people are finding faith and lives are changing, but infection remains, unless there is a miracle. For example a drug addict who is HIV + will join a growing church once he becomes a practising Christian.

'It could never happen here'

In parts of central Africa it seems that one in five of all the young men and women are already doomed by the virus. We now know that AIDS was around in Africa, as in the USA, back as early as the 1960s. People were dying, but even with all the medical teams alerted, we only realised there was a single case of AIDS in Africa in 1983. In that year we suddenly began to realise the silent disaster in central Africa. It was possible that tens of thousands had already perished, and millions were already infected. For them it was too late.

Now AIDS is threatening parts of Asia in a similar way.

In Mumbai alone over 1,000 new people are infected every night. I have visited villages in NE India on the Burmese border where out of around 40,000 people, 8,000 inject heroin and 4,000 are infected. I sat on the bed with the dying son of a pastor whose oldest brother had already been killed by HIV. Whole generations are being devastated. And yet as we will see, there is a very simple answer that costs nothing and saves millions of lives every year.

Worse than a war

If everyone infected with HIV survived only six weeks, the USA would be in national mourning and the economy would be in a state of collapse. There would be mass panic. Vietnam wiped out 50,000 American young men from the US army over ten years. With over a million HIV infections in the US so far, AIDS makes those war deaths look almost insignificant. Even if there is not a single new infection in the USA after the moment you buy this book, the death toll will be the equivalent of twenty Vietnam wars.

And in Africa? We know that armed conflict encourages spread. Most wars today are wars inside nations rather than between them, causing millions of refugees to flee. When law and order breaks down and armed militia roam the streets or spring out of the bush to halt traffic, it becomes impossible to run a health service or pay for it. Prevention campaigns collapse and disease spreads. Ill-disciplined groups of armed men often have many sexual partners, either at gunpoint or in return for favours. All these things mean HIV spreads even faster.

Some informal reports suggest the rate of HIV infection in the Kenya army is up to 90% among some groups. We know that many communities in South Africa are already badly hit with up to one in five infected. This is a pandemic with unimaginable impact on hundreds of millions of people.

So who is safe then?

You are safe from AIDS if you are not infected yourself and are faithful, to one partner, who is also not infected at the moment and remains loyal to you and does not take risks with injecting, or with unsafe medical treatments.

Nothing new about AIDS?

Sex diseases have been around for thousands of years. Syphilis infected and killed tens of thousands of people until a treatment was found forty years ago. Gonorrhoea has continued to spread rapidly and is now often resistant to our drugs. We have a big problem with herpes which causes painful blisters, making sex impossible. It comes and goes for life. There is no cure. Cancer of the neck of the womb (cervix) is becoming more common because you are more likely to get it if you first have sex as a teenager and have a number of different partners. More and more women are also finding they can't have children. This is increasingly because of sex diseases, which damage a woman inside. Usually she doesn't realise until the damage is done.

The great sex age is over

In the sixties in the West people talked a lot about sexual liberation once the pill meant that a woman was safe from getting pregnant. In the seventies, eighties and nineties there was an explosion of sexual activity among young people in many nations, and the number of young people needing treatment for sex diseases soared.

We are now living with the results of the sex age where long-term relationships have not been as important as having a good time tonight, where many people have stopped thinking twice before jumping into bed together or before cheating on each other, and where marriage built on faithfulness has often become meaningless.

But what has it all left us with? Our so-called 'wonderful' sex age has left us with millions of casualties; young people who have grown up in households that have fallen to pieces because a parent has had several partners. You don't have to be a doctor or a child psychiatrist to see what a disaster it has been for so many today.

People are also having second thoughts because of AIDS.

Chapter Two

Vaccines, Treatments and Condoms

No one dies solely of AIDS

AIDS is a condition when a particular virus has weakened your body so other germs can invade and kill you. That's what the name 'AIDS' means: your body is usually very good at destroying germs. We call this immunity. When your immune defences are badly damaged, we say you are suffering from an immune deficiency. Some people are born with bad immune systems and others acquire a deficiency because of a disease. Because AIDS is acquired through an infection, we call it the Acquired Immune Deficiency Syndrome (AIDS for short).

HIV just stands for Human Immune-deficiency Virus, which is the scientific name for the virus which causes AIDS.

Whatever names we use, one thing is important and

that is to realise that there are stages from being infected, where a person is an infectious carrier but well, through to early symptoms, and then finally to more severe illness or death. The process takes years. It is totally impossible to tell by appearances who is infectious and who is not.

What is a virus?

A virus is just like a robot or a computer programme. It simply contains some written directions to teach cells in your body how to make more viruses. A virus is made up of a bag of protein with a small strip of genetic code inside it. This is like the code that makes your hair brown, your nose and your ears the shape they are. Everything inside you is programmed by these genes, and amazingly almost every cell in your body has inside it all the instructions to make a complete copy of you!

The code inside the virus only contains one or two instructions, but wrong ones. If the virus sticks for more than a moment onto the outside of a special type of white blood cell, the virus bursts like a tiny bubble, squirting the lethal code into the cell. Within a few minutes the cell has taken a copy inside the cell brain (nucleus) and the cell brain has been permanently reprogrammed. This cell is doomed.

Killing off the soldier cells

For a few weeks or months, or even for a few years, the infected soldier cell keeps floating around in the blood, or swimming between the tissues of your body. The cell has one aim in life: locate and destroy germs. There are hundreds of different germs and each kind of white cell is designed to attack one kind of germ.

Why you get ill

Only certain kinds of soldier cells get attacked by the virus, but as they get fewer and fewer it gets harder and harder for your body to kill certain germs. You are fine with ordinary coughs and colds. Most common germs are quickly destroyed, but one or two just keep on growing. The result is a strange chest infection, TB or other illnesses.

When a soldier cell meets the right shaped germ it springs into action. After being sleepy for years it works overtime to help produce antibodies. These fit exactly onto the outside of the germ and destroy it. But if the cell has been reprogrammed, the mechanism gets jammed. The new programme jumps into action and tells the cell to stop helping to make antibodies. Instead it starts to make new viruses. The cell gets sicker as it gets larger. Eventually it bursts, showering millions more virus particles into the blood. Each one stays in the blood for only a few minutes before it touches a fresh healthy white cell, bursts, injects the code and reprogrammes new cells — soldier cells and brain cells, for example. After a while the body is weakened and other infections start to take over.

Some of these infections simply cause you to feel run down or to lose weight, but the chest infections can kill and are very hard to treat. No one dies solely of AIDS. You die largely because of the other infections that take over your body when your defences are damaged, or from cancers related to HIV. TB is a common killer of people with advanced HIV infection.

Newsflash on Cures, Vaccines and Condoms

Almost every week it seems we read or hear about some new wonder cure for AIDS. They say someone has already found a vaccine, and they also tell us how sex is safe if you use a condom. These things are good news if they are true — but are they? Some say that if you have sex with a virgin you will be cured. Nonsense. It is amazing what people will believe.

A lot of what you read and hear is rubbish. If it was as easy as some people make out to find a cure, or if a good vaccine really had been found, doctors, nurses, hospitals and governments could stop worrying. The reason why there is so much fuss about preventing the spread of infection is because the truth is that there is no cure, nor is there one anywhere in sight. There is no vaccine that works, nor is there likely to be one for at least ten years. To make it worse, condoms are much less safe than some people think they are.

I hope that soon we will have a drug that kills viruses and is safe. When that happens, we will have a cure for flu, the common cold, polio, hepatitis, herpes and many other illnesses such as glandular fever; as well as a cure for AIDS. It is a long way off.

At the moment we don't have the technology to do it. Making a cure will involve us inventing some amazing tools that will allow us to work inside individual cells in the body. Landing a man on the moon or even on Mars is very simple compared to the skills needed to find a cure. The person who finds a cure will go down in history books as one of the greatest inventors of all time. Books will be written about him or her well into the twenty-second century.

In the meantime you will read of hundreds of false 'cures'. The trouble with AIDS is that people who have it don't actually die of AIDS alone. As we have seen, they die of the infections and problems that come in when AIDS has weakened the body. Anything that helps the body get rid of these other infections can help someone make a dramatic recovery. They go home looking well, and are sometimes still completely well some months later. Until they get another chest infection, people think they have been cured. This gives rise to rumours and false reports:

'I took this special antibiotic and within a day I was out of hospital and haven't looked back since. I don't have AIDS any more.'

The first comment is right, the second is wrong. The person could die quite quickly at any time. The soldier cells are getting weaker and weaker, and with each passing day the body is more and more wide open to new germs. Although the person may be looking well, he or she is sitting on a time-bomb.

Rubbish cures

In India many indigenous treatments are being advertised as cures for HIV, such as herbal remedies and other therapies.

In Uganda a few years back, drugs for tuberculosis were being talked about as a cure for AIDS. Nonsense. People with AIDS are especially likely to die of tuberculosis. The drug kills tuberculosis, not AIDS. In the USA, treatments for syphilis have been called treatments for AIDS. They are not — they help people recover from syphilis alone.

Some people are pushing fad diets, whole-meal foods, vitamins in large doses, exercise, sleep and psychotherapy in varying combinations as a cure for AIDS. What value do these things have?

It is true that if your soldier cells aren't working too well then anything that helps your immunity is going to help keep you healthy, and things which make you run down and prone to being ill should be avoided. Common sense tells you to take care of yourself. Eat proper regular meals, take some exercise, keep your weight reasonable, eat plenty of fresh fruit, cut out the smoking, cut down on alcohol and stop all other recreational drugs and make sure you get enough sleep. These low-cost measures are likely to prolong the life and well-being of most people and especially of those with AIDS or early HIV infection.

However, some people are advertising all kinds of very expensive and useless remedies. A lot of people are making a lot of money out of AIDS.

Effective Treatment

It's true that there are some medicines available called HIV protease inhibitors and other things. But these just damp down the fire, they don't put it out. They are all poisonous so you can die from over-treatment and that means many hospital tests. The medicines have to be taken for life and can be very expensive, although prices are falling and treatment is free in some parts of the world.

Until recently, a Burundi doctor would have had to save his entire salary for five years to pay for treatment and monitoring of just one person on these drugs for one year — and the person would still die of AIDS in the end. Because of this there has been a huge outcry for justice and the manufacturers have taken steps to provide the drugs at much lower cost. But to people on Rs.100 a day of income, it is still far too costly.

Just as the idea that everyone in the poorest nations can afford to use condoms when they have sex, it is also stupid to pretend that these lower cost drugs will make any difference at all to the poorest people. This is why the World Health Organisation launched a new global initiative in 2003, aiming to provide free antiviral medicines to at least 3 million people ill because of HIV, by 2005 (3 by 5 programme). This ambitious programme will only reach targets by working closely with churches and Christian organisations, who as we have seen are   major providers of care in the poorest nations. Those who test positive after pretest counselling, and are unwell with symptoms suggesting AIDS will be started on combination tablets containing more than one antiretroviral medicine, with simple blood tests every two weeks to make sure their bodies are able to use the medicine safely (see back of book on how to get free WHO AIDS treatment). But this is still not a cure and the treatment itself can make people ill or even die.

What about a vaccine?

Vaccines are our only weapons against viral diseases. Polio, whooping cough, measles and other illnesses are becoming more rare now thanks to vaccines. A worldwide programme against smallpox has now succeeded in wiping it off the face of the earth. So why not AIDS?

A vaccine is made by giving you a germ that is harmless but is the same shape on the outside as the disease germ. Within a week you will develop special antibodies to get rid of it. The first time it always takes longer. The next time you meet the same germ, it takes only an hour or two to get your soldier cells into battle. Your soldier cells can remember a germ they have met before several years ago.

If you now meet a completely different and dangerous germ, and the shape is the same as a germ your body has met previously, your body is well prepared, and instead of dying of polio, for example, you feel slightly unwell and get better in a day or two. The vaccine has made you immune.

Master of disguise

The trouble with AIDS is that the virus keeps changing its shape so it confuses the soldier cells. A vaccine you give someone today might protect him or her next week, but what about next month? Here we have a virus that is immune to your soldier cells. That is why your body can virtually never get rid of it. There are other viruses that change shape as well. You may have wondered why flu is still a major cause of lost days at work or at school, or why all our skills are defeated by the common cold.

The reason is that both of these illnesses are caused by viruses that tend to look a bit different every time you meet them. By the time you have passed your cold on to a friend, and it has been passed on another few dozen times, it has travelled halfway round the world, infected maybe 10,000 people in total, and has altered shape. Each person infected makes new viruses inside their nose cells and sometimes the viruses coming out are not exactly the same shape as the virus that came in.

A year or two later you meet someone with a cold — the same cold you had before. If the virus were like measles or chickenpox, your body would have remembered it and killed it straight away. But the virus looks so different on the outside that when the soldier cells get their picture library out, they just can't identify it. There is no pre-made antibody that is a good enough fit, so the soldier cells have to start all over again.

A vaccine for flu

There is a vaccine for flu and it just about works because the virus tends to stay the same shape for a bit longer than the cold virus. We have a look at what's coming round the corner from the other side of the world. We take samples from people in Hong Kong and Australia and we know that if we can get the vaccines made and give it quickly to old people in Canada then we may be able to reduce the number of flu deaths this winter. But you have to have a new vaccine each year.

So even if we do find a vaccine for AIDS which is safe and works, we will probably have to revaccinate everyone at frequent intervals. The virus may still not be destroyed. It can change shape in small ways even in the same person over a few weeks, so antibodies that were a good fit at the beginning of the month are almost useless by the end of the month.

A virus dressed up to look like you

Whatever you may read, the truth is that we have never

yet found a single human antibody that is powerful against HIV - even if it is exactly the right shape. Almost everyone who is infected produces antibodies, but they still get ill and die. This virus is immune to antibodies.

So when you next hear of some wonderful scientist who has given himself a dose of AIDS vaccine, take care. The only way we will know if it works is by giving him an injection of blood from someone who has AIDS and seeing what happens. But how long do you think you will have to wait to be absolutely sure that he will never develop AIDS? Possibly ten years. Until then his wife and children will be living in suspense, knowing that he might die, and also that he may be an infectious carrier.

Give him a test?

You may ask why we can't give him an AIDS test. Unfortunately, the AIDS test is nothing of the sort. It is extremely difficult to detect this tiny virus. The only widely available test we have at the moment is not for the virus itself, but for the antibodies that almost all infected people make. So people wanting a test often have to wait a while after they were last at risk before being tested — up to twelve weeks. If we find antibodies, it means that the person has been exposed to the infection — or that he or she has developed antibodies because of a vaccine. We cannot tell the difference.

Most experts are very depressed when it comes to talking about vaccines. They say that we are almost certainly at least ten years from a vaccine that works, and even if we find one it will take years to make sure it is safe enough to give to large numbers of people and to produce at low cost in large quantities.

Condoms are not the whole answer to AIDS

Many churches don't like talking about condoms at

all. But what is the truth? Are condoms the medical answer? Is promoting the use of condoms something that is opposed to the values of Christ? And another question...

If AIDS kills, the body can't fight it, drugs don't really touch it and vaccines are as good as useless, then what hope is there? Whenever I go into schools or talk to young people they all tell me that safe sex is sex with a condom — even though they may have also decided never to use one. But even if they were to change their minds and to use condoms, do they really work as well as people make out? Something no one likes to tell you is that condoms may not be as safe as you think they are.

Here is the truth:

Condoms can reduce the risk of HIV spreading enormously but they are not 100% safe.

And here is a concern:

Sometimes indiscriminate promotion of condoms can give a mixed message to young people: on the one hand encouraging them to be celibate and then faithful, and on the other seeming perhaps to encourage them to have multiple partners in situations where they could be exposed to infection unless they use a condom.

Everyone agrees that one major thing more than any other produced the sexual explosion of the swinging sixties, with liberation of women from the fear of pregnancy, the ability to plan a family reliably, and to explore free sexual relationships. The swinging sixties were produced by the pill not the condom.

Condom babies

Before the sixties every mother warned her daughter that if she slept around she could land up with a baby she didn't want. Condoms have been around for years — since

1850 BC (not AD), in fact. The ancient Chinese and the Romans knew all about condoms and they were no more reliable then.

During the Second World War condoms were freely available in many countries and were the main form of contraception, yet 'war babies', born to women after hasty affairs with soldiers on leave, became a standing joke. Thousands of parents and grandparents and aunts and uncles today were born as 'war babies', or after the war, as 'condom babies'. These were babies that surprised and shocked young girls who thought they were safe from pregnancy because their boyfriends or husbands were wearing condoms.

Even today the success of the latest condoms is not as good as many people think when it comes to reliably preventing pregnancy. If, as a doctor, I have 100 young women patients who have chosen the condom to prevent themselves having babies, then each year I can expect maybe fourteen of the 100 to come into the surgery in a state of shock and confusion because they have missed periods, but just can't believe they are pregnant because their partners were using condoms.

Holey condoms!

Just for the record, condoms on sale, which are poor quality can have up to seven out of ten with holes in them, faults when you open the packet. The best have only one in 200 with a hole in before you start. But what happens after you open the packet is far more important. It can be quite difficult to use a condom correctly. Fumbling in the dark it can be torn, caught in a woman's jewellery, it can burst, fall off, roll off and leak if not removed carefully at the end of making love.

If we are honest we have to say that no one is quite sure why condoms have such an appalling habit of letting you down. One good reason may be that people who say they are using them, do buy them with good intentions, but when it actually comes to the heat of the moment they don't get as far as putting them on.

You can get infected even with a condom

If you were to draw a sperm and a virus on the same scale, then if a sperm were ten centimetres long, a virus would be the size of a pinhead. If sperm can cross from a man to a woman, then viruses can too. They can also cross from a woman to a man. It is not surprising then to find that reports are now coming in of men who have infected their wives, or the other way round, with the HIV virus, despite using condoms carefully.

Even if a condom fails, a woman is unlikely to get pregnant. You can only get pregnant on three out of thirty days a month, and even if it happens to be a day when there is an egg around to be fertilised, many people have to try many times before a baby is conceived. In fact five in 100 people will never manage it. Another five in 100 will take months or years of anxious trying before they succeed in having a baby. Mr and Mrs Average take around four months of trying.

But with HIV, you can in theory get infected any day of the month. Once can be enough to get it from him or from her.

Condoms are like seat-belts

Seat-belts save thousands of lives a year, but it is feared that because people feel safer wearing them they actually encourage speeding, jumping lights and crazy overtaking. In the end people may land up in riskier situations, and the number of lives saved may not be as great as it should have been.

Condoms are exactly the same: they reduce your

chance of dying from an activity which can be highly dangerous. By pushing condoms and making out they are more reliable than they are, some health campaigns may actually encourage people not to alter the way they live. 'Carry on as normal, but just remember, when you can, to use a condom.'

It is very simple: if you are going to take a risk by having sex with someone who could be infected (and how will you ever know, since people don't tell the truth and you can't tell by looking) and you don't use a condom, you are crazy.

A condom may well save your life. Condoms have without a doubt saved millions of people from dying of AIDS already.

When using condoms, make sure they are good quality. Condoms can deteriorate in hot countries if kept for many months before use. In conjunction, use a spermicide containing nonoxynol to reduce risk further. If you want to use a lubricant, use those which are water based and contain nonoxynol spermicide. Oil-based lubricants can rot condoms in minutes.

But don't kid yourself that just because you use a condom there will never be a baby or you will never become infected.

If you are having sex regularly with someone, or with people who are carrying the virus, then one day, condom or no condom, you may get infected. It is the same as someone who enjoys driving a fast sports car beyond the limits of road — safety, thinking he could never be killed in an accident because he always wears a seat-belt. The seat-belt makes him safer — but it does not guarantee he won't get hurt.

You can't have an abortion for AIDS

Condoms reduce the risk by about 85-95%, but I wouldn't trust my life to a condom. There are people who are infected or have died, despite using them. Condoms are not as safe as some of you think. All the health literature says that 'for safer sex use a condom'. The trouble is that we hear what we want to hear. We hear 'safe'. As someone said recently, you can abort a baby, but you can't have an abortion for AIDS.

Condoms can be worn by women

There are some new kinds of condoms available now. They are made of the same material as ordinary condoms, but with reinforcement to keep them in place inside a woman. They can provide an added measure of protection. The trouble is that when a man and woman are actually making love, these very thin membranes of rubber, whether worn by a man or a woman, can slip or move. Things happen, and neither partner is aware until afterwards when it is too late. The stronger and thicker you make these things, the less and less people want to have anything to do with them. The ideal condom is invisible, with neither partner aware at all of anything feeling any different. It doesn't exist, although some say the female condom is an improvement, and it can be reused many times. 3.5 crore have been sold worldwide.

Condoms must be part of the Christian answer to AIDS

Churches take very different positions on the condom issue but however anti-condom a church may be, consider this: a man comes to the pastor because he has been infected through a blood transfusion and is worried about the health of his wife. Both have been tested. He is infected but she is not. What advice will he be given? Surely the only advice that makes sense is for both husband and wife to understand that there is a serious risk to her life if they have unprotected sex, but that if they use a condom carefully, every time they make love, it will reduce the risk of her getting infected enormously. In such a situation it would be madness, almost perhaps an act of murder, not to inform the couple of the real benefits of condom use.

In such a situation let us work out the risks. We know that if both partners are healthy, apart from one having HIV, that is to say if neither have untreated syphilis, gonorrhea, chancroid or another chronic sexually transmitted disease, then in normal heterosexual intercourse, the chances of transmitting HIV during a single episode is probably less than one in 200. And we know that using a condom may reduce this risk further by 90% or more. That means that the risk of getting HIV from your husband or wife if you are using condoms carefully in such a situation is probably less than one in 2000. In other words, on average such a couple would need to make love 2000 times before the uninfected partner gets HIV. Of course it could happen after just twenty times, or not even after 10,000 times. It's an average figure that you would get by following up what happens to hundreds of couples.

So for a Christian it seems obvious that in some circumstances at least there should be no reservations whatsoever about the use of a condom where the aim is to save the life of a husband or wife in marriage. How much further we go down this route depends on the church and as I say traditions and cultures vary hugely.

Dilemmas for engaged couples

Incidentally, some church leaders in badly affected countries are saying that they will not marry couples unless they have been tested, and if one or both have HIV they forbid them to marry. But I cannot find a bible passage that supports such action. Clearly we should encourage people to be very caring and responsible. If both man and woman have HIV I cannot see any reason medically why they should not marry, any more than two people with cancer. Most likely they will think very carefully before attempting to have children, partly because of the risk of infecting them, even though HIV drugs can reduce that risk if taken in pregnancy. But partly also because of the risk to the welfare of the child if orphaned at a young age.

An engaged couple where one is infected and the other is not are in a terrible situation, because they are entering a life-long relationship where the act of greatest intimacy could kill one of them. But even so it seems to me that these things are matters of sensitive personal counsel and cannot be made absolute rules of the church.

What about smoking?

I was recently debating this whole issue of condoms with many church leaders in Burundi. I asked them if they approved of smoking. They said no. I pointed out that you can smoke cigarettes with filters or without but filtered cigarettes are far safer, they kill less people. So if they had a friend who insisted on smoking, would they encourage them to smoke filtered cigarettes? Would they explain how much safer it was? Or would they feel it was just encouraging people to smoke even more?

They agreed that however much they were against smoking, the last thing they would want is for cigarettes to be even more dangerous and they would agree that government advertising should explain that smokers are better off using filtered brands.

I pointed out it was in many ways the same kind of argument with condoms. If someone is going to take a risk anyway (despite all our persuasions), and could lose their life as a result of having sex with an infected partner tonight, don't we have the same obligation to warn them of the risks, and explain how to avoid a slow death sentence?

So for me the issue is clear: we do all we can to

encourage celibacy and faithfulness, but we also make people aware that there is a way of reducing the risk of death, if they choose to go their own way.

Condoms are very costly for poor nations to give to everyone

There is another problems with condoms: cost. Only the female condom can be used more than once safely. So who is going to supply them?

ACET International Alliance — the network of AIDS programmes in many nations that I helped found in 1988 — was once offered 140 million Chinese condoms delivered to any port in Africa for a certain price. I told them that even if we had the money, I calculated that 140 million condoms would last the continent of Africa just one night — and then what would people do? And what is more it would wipe out our entire budget for HIV for a very long time. Even the World Health Organisation does not have enough money to fund such schemes on a sustainable basis. The Health Minister in Uganda was offered half a million condoms by a wealthy business man in 1990 and had the same reaction: "thanks very much but it will last our country a day". We have to think more deeply than pieces of rubber. We have to face reality. We have to think on a far larger and longer scale.

Condoms may be a solution for wealthy people, able to buy as many as they need, or for those fortunate enough to live near a free distribution point but one thing is clear: wealthy nations are unwilling and unable to pay out enough money for every sexual act to be thus protected in the 2/3rds world, so the idea that we should just tell everyone to use condoms is a cruel joke. And when 200 crore people exist on incomes of less than Rs.100 a day, living in countries like India where the health budget is only Rs.100 a person for a whole year, how can condoms be a sustainable and affordable, locally appropriate solution?

Condoms have to be produced in high-tech factories, to high standards, packaged carefully, and stored well. That's why they are expensive and an odd "Western-style" solution for a low-tech society where many villagers may have very few manufactured items: a plastic water container, a couple of metal cooking pans, a battery radio and the clothes they wear. Everything else is produced locally from what grows or is dug from the earth. Are we really expecting condoms to be the answer in places like this? Of course, condoms also have an advantage of providing birth control for those that want it, but the practical issues remain.

HIV is a development issue

That's one of the reasons we conclude that HIV is a development issue. Poverty encourages spread. Ignorance, lack of health care, poor communications, destitution, children earning money or food from casual sex, and so on. These cycles of deprivation need to be broken together. Just focussing on HIV will not itself succeed in halting AIDS.

Take for example an infected commercial sex worker: how is she to live if she stops providing her services to men? Who will feed her children? Who will pay for her medicines? Prevention campaigns are not enough. We need a holistic approach.

That's why one of the weapons against HIV is economic growth: encouraging investment, business and international trade. Microbanking, income-generation schemes, and other self-help programmes have a vital role to play, not only in raising general incomes in a nation, but also in helping those with HIV rebuild their lives and helping orphans survive. I have seen 40,000 people lifted simultaneously out of absolute poverty in places like Delhi:

people who had been in tents and slum dwellings now living in two storeyed houses with all facilities, and with successful businesses, largely as a result of microbanking schemes, where groups of women take out small loans together for several businesses and guarantee each other.

As we have seen, AIDS is a terrible disease for which there is no cure and no vaccine. The only hope is to teach people how to protect themselves from infection. If there is no cure, no vaccine, and condoms merely reduce the risk as well as being unaffordable or unavailable for crores of people, what is the answer?

Experience in Africa

Just a few weeks ago I flew to a country where a solution has been urgently needed to prevent a big part of a whole generation from being wiped out. Uganda has had in the past more reported cases of AIDS than any other country in Africa. You might think that means it is the worst affected: it is not. It is certainly the country with the most honest and courageous leaders. And it has had one of the most successful campaigns in the world with dramatic results.

There were several other African nations that had as bad a problem, or maybe even worse, who would not speak up. One country actually reduced the number of AIDS cases it admitted to, even though doctors in that country knew the figures were fixed. If people think you have a lot of AIDS then big companies pull out and tourists stop coming. The economy collapses and in addition to having thousands of extra sick young people to look after, you now have high unemployment and increasing poverty.

The government of Uganda openly admitted there was a big problem. This opened the doors for international aid and also for education. How can you educate people about a major cause of death when you don't officially admit anyone is actually dying of it?

In some parts of central Africa, one in three of all the truck drivers who drive lorries up and down the main highways are infected, and half the young girls who hang around the bars at night. Maybe one in five of all young men and women in some of these towns are infected. Some have said they think there are towns in central Africa where maybe half of all the sexually active young people are dying.

Like any other sex disease

I met a mother who had lost two daughters. Her face was a picture of grief. Composed and dignified, she told me how they had died. 'I wish it had been me,' she said, 'they were so young.' In Africa the infection has always spread like any other sex disease: from man to woman and woman to man. Europeans who stay in these countries often come home infected after having had sex only a few times.

In 1988 I visited Uganda for the first time: we spoke to over 20,000 people in around ten days, at the request and invitation of the Ministries of Health and Education. When we went into schools and asked for a show of hands from those who knew personally of people who had died because of AIDS, half would put up their hands. Two years later it was almost everyone.

We held large open-air meetings with a big noisy African band, a huge public address system and interpreters. Thousands attended from local villages. Up to 2,500 people sat in the square or stood motionless, six deep for around three hours, while we assisted the local people in educating and answering questions. Most of the audience were men — hardly ever turning up to such things normally. They came because in the area where we were, AIDS had become a life and death issue for everyone there.

Desperate for a test

Many young people came to me wanting to be tested. They had good reason to be worried. They knew there was a very high chance that either of two people about to get married could be infected. If they both are, that is one thing, but if not, then one could kill the other. What should they do? It is quite feeble just to tell them to use condoms carefully for the rest of their lives.

What about children? If the girl has a baby, she knows that the infection can be passed in the milk. She wants to be tested to make sure she does not accidentally kill her baby. A wife came to me. She was worried because her husband was often out with other women late at night. He admitted he had been repeatedly unfaithful over the last ten years, and they both realised that he could easily be infected, like so many of the people he knew who had died. They wanted to know if it was safe for him to sleep with anyone again — let alone his wife.

All these anxious people: they do not only need counselling. Some of them have an urgent need for a test. Testing is one of the most powerful weapons we have in the fight against AIDS because it helps identify people who are carrying the virus so they can take steps not to kill others and receive effective treatment. It also helps other people discover that they and their partners are not infected, so they can enjoy anxiety-free, condom-free sex for life with no risk whatever of HIV unless one or other is unfaithful.

One partner for life

The response of the Ugandan government to the crisis was prompt and impressive. No watered down messages. For them the answer was obvious and clear: 'Safe sex is sex between virgins now married for life. (If you really can't manage it a condom might save your life.)'

In Africa many governments have been very worried too about spread from medical treatments. In some areas one in five bottles of blood donated to the hospital blood banks is full of virus. Fortunately almost everywhere now in Africa they have facilities to test all blood. Needles can also be in short supply, or equipment to heat and sterilise can be broken or unavailable. No one will ever know just how many doctors and nurses have been killed in Africa without knowing it. So an important part of the health campaign has been making sure that everyone is aware of the dangers of blood and needles.

People say Africa is different

A lot of people have tried to think up various reasons why Africa is different. You must make up your own mind. Some said that Africans are especially sensitive to HIV and that is why it spread so fast. They worked out that answer from experience in a London clinic. For six months that was the answer trotted out around the world, until the doctors made a public confession that they had wrongly added up the figures.

The next answer given was that Africans are much more promiscuous. People believe what they like to believe. While it is certainly true that some patterns of behaviour encourage multiple sexual partners in parts of Africa, the difference is not enough to explain what is happening.

Another suggestion was that medical treatments with dirty, needles and infected blood was the reason. It is easy to make armchair assessments when you are 6,000 miles away. The fact is that if that were true then every age group that receives medical care by injection would be likely to get AIDS, whereas most of those infected are young sexually-active men and women.

Finally, some suggested that infection first with one disease could open the body to infection by another. We have very strong reasons to think this happens. Common sense tells us that if you are already chronically sick and then you are infected by the AIDS virus, you are not in the best possible shape to fight it. Malaria and other tropical diseases could be responsible.

However, the most likely explanation is other sex diseases. These spread in all countries but chronic untreated STDs are far more common in poorer nations where there are fewer health care facilities. In addition, tracing sexual partners of those infected can be harder in nations with less well-organised community systems. We do know that if a man or a woman is infected with gonorrhoea or syphilis or similar diseases, the small wounds made by these germs become easy ways into the body for the AIDS virus.

One of the reasons that HIV is spreading so fast in places like Mumbai in India is that around half of all adults in that vast city are carrying an active untreated STD.

You can see for yourself that everything that has happened in central Africa is bound to happen to some extent in the West. It is a stupid man who comes back from a detailed look at what is happening in Africa and says AIDS will never affect people other than gay men and drug addicts in the UK. Not only stupid but ignorant too: in 2001 the majority of people newly infected in the UK were heterosexuals — and mostly infected in other nations.

How can I keep uninfected ?

You may want to make a decision if you have not already done so, that the next person you have sex with will be the person you are committed to making love to for the rest of your life. Some say life is not that simple. What if that person has had several partners before, or what if you have? What if your partner is unfaithful or is injecting drugs?

The question of testing is a difficult and complex one and every person or couple is different. Where the risk is significant it may well be worth one or both being tested for the sake of the other. You need expert medical advice from your doctor or from a special clinic.

The other decision to make, if you have not already done so, is never, never under any circumstances to allow yourself to be injected with a needle that could contain traces of someone else's blood.

Zero risk

If you keep to these two very simple things you will reduce your risk to nearly zero. Any remaining risk would be if your partner was continuing to take risks — especially if you are kept in the dark - or if you are in the medical or caring professions. If you fall into this group you should already have clear instructions on how to protect yourself while also giving excellent care. The basic rule is to keep blood and any other body fluids off your skin as far as possible.

In the next chapter we look at some of the common worries and problems people have.

Chapter Three

Agony AIDS

The trouble with AIDS is that most people are far too scared to ask the things they really need answers to.

'My boyfriend says that I don't love him because I don't want to have sex with him.'

One thing is absolutely certain: he doesn't love you — or if he does, he doesn't respect you. If he is pressurising you to give yourself to him with no real commitment on his part, he is more interested in getting pleasure for himself than in building a relationship with you.

'I know my boyfriend and he says he's a virgin too, so it must be safe.'

A man will tell you anything he wants in order to have sex with you, if he wants it enough. The world is full of hurt girls and women who have been badly let down. They agreed to have sex as a way of tying him down, out of fear that the relationship would break up, because he promised that they would get married one day. But he had no intention whatsoever of getting 'trapped for life'.

You may be looking for a home, a husband who will love you, care for you and be a good dad to your children. But your boyfriend may be just looking for a good time, no strings attached, and a relationship can turn off like a tap when one day he sees someone new or gets bored. In the meantime you will hear everything you have dreamed of hearing: 'I love you. You are the only girl for me. I am committed to you.'

Anyway, even if he is a virgin now, do you really think that he is never going to sleep with any other girl for the rest of his life? Is this really it? Is he really the guy who is never going to look at another girl again? If he is so keen to have sex with you now before any commitment in marriage, he'll be just as keen to try it out with someone else later on, even maybe after he has married you.

'The two of us are getting married next year. We have not had sex together. But both of us, if we're honest, have had a bit of a past. Should we both be tested before we get married?'

This is a really urgent issue for many couples now, especially in Africa where the risks of marrying someone who is infected are enormous. Many people ask to be tested for these reasons. I think there is a good case for it. It depends on how big the risk has been. A member of a church came up to me the other day. He had been an injector of heroin until a few years ago when became a Christian, which changed his entire life and he broke the habit. Should he be tested before going any further?

These questions need expert individual counselling. There is no standard right answer. As a general rule, if it is possible that you or your future partner may have been exposed to HIV then you will both want to be tested out of love and care for each other. How terrible it would be to kill the one you love. Many churches in countries where AIDS is a big problem are now refusing to marry people without HIV tests first.

And what of the results? If both are negative then that is wonderful news. If one is positive and the other is negative then the consequencies of marriage could be very serious. I am not saying they should not be allowed to marry. This seems to me to be a personal choice, but they do need to understand the risks. It will mean very careful use of a condom every time they make love, and finding other ways to express intimacy and affection other than full intercourse. It will mean (probably) a decision not to have children since having a baby would carry a real risk of killing the future mother or father. If both are already infected, then there is no reason for them not to marry, since they are not going to kill each other by transmitting the virus. They will still have a dilemma over whether or not to have children, with the risk of an infected child or a child being orphaned at a young age.

The best person to talk over HIV testing with is a specialized advisor at a clinic for genito - urinary diseases (STDs). Most major hospitals have them. You usually don't need an appointment, and they will respect complete confidence — they have to, otherwise no one would ever go to them.

'In a country like India, where marriages are arranged by both families, is there a relevance for the two individuals getting married to be tested for HIV before the wedding takes place?'

If either partner has been at risk this is important, but it can be culturally very sensitive to talk about.

'How infectious is HIV?'

HIV is much less infectious than for example hepatitis B. Let us suppose there is an accident while a doctor is taking blood from someone with HIV and he pricks himself with the needle. We know from many such events that   infection is unusual as a result — it is a risk of one in 200 or more. So a doctor would need to have around 200 accidents like that on average before becoming infected himself, because the amount of HIV you need is quite high to get an infection. But with hepatitis B a doctor would only need to have 5 accidents on average to get infected.

Now if it is the case that the risk is only one in 200 even when you are jabbed by a medical needle, you can see that the risk from — say — a splash of blood onto your hand is very, very small indeed. Intact skin is usually a brilliant barrier against HIV. But a squirt of blood into the eye can be dangerous. So is injecting drugs like heroin with shared equipment, where the previous person's blood is mixed up into the next person's injection.

During normal sexual intercourse between a man and a woman, the risk is around one in 200 of infection from a single episode of unprotected sex with an infected partner who is well, without symptoms. But if one or other has another untreated sex disease such as chancroid or gonorrhoea, and the person may not realise, nor their partner, then the risk of transmission could be ten or twenty times higher. This is also true if the person is ill with AIDS.

So then HIV is far less infectious than most people realise. If that's the case, why does it spread so fast in many places? The reason is that although the risk of an individual act may be quite low, when the same act is repeated over and over again, or where many millions of people are involved, the numbers of risks taken is beyond counting and the virus has a huge number of chances to cross from one person to another.

'In the Indian or African situation if a husband is infected and the wife is not and the husband insists on having sex with his wife, what is the advice given?'

This is a very serious situation which could kill the wife and can be culturally very difficult if the woman is powerless. At the very least out of love and respect for his wife, and to protect children from losing both parents, one hopes the husband will use a condom.

'I am confused because many people say certain things can give you AIDS and other people say they cannot.'

It is very confusing for people, and most people, most of the time, are more afraid of the stories than anything else. Can I get AIDS from a cup, or what about kissing, or swimming, or mosquitoes or anything else? Before answering all these questions in detail, we need to look at the kind of dangers we put ourselves in every day.

Each time you travel in a car or a bus you could die in a crash, and on a bus you could catch flu. You could get bitten by a dog and mugged on the way home from work. The world can be a dangerous place, but we have to get things in proportion or we would all worry ourselves sick. Some people get overwhelmed by all these things and get, so worked up that they cannot go outside the house. They need expert help. Others laugh at them: 'Surely people realise that the risk of something dreadful happening is incredibly small?'

When it comes to AIDS, even the most sensible of us can start behaving in a very odd manner. A grown man leaves a parcel in the rain at the door of the house because he is afraid to speak to anyone inside. A community worker is afraid to drink her cup of tea. At church people are staying away from communion services because they are afraid of the common cup — even though it is safe. At a conference very few want to shake the hand of a visiting speaker.

A few years ago the ACET community care team with whom I worked needed urgently to find bigger offices. After much searching we found somewhere ideal, but the owners were afraid we would pollute the toilets and refused to let us move in.

The trouble is that if I told you that many of these things had absolutely no risk you probably would not believe me. If I told you there was in fact a risk you will probably spend the rest of your life worrying. I am not interested in alarming or comforting you. I do want you to know the facts so you can make up your own mind. So we will now look at a few examples:

'I read in a paper that an expert had said you could get AIDS by eating a meal. Is this true or not?'

No! I suppose that in theory if an infected waiter was to cut his finger with a sharp knife, and hold his finger while it dripped fresh blood all over your meal, and then after he put it in front of you, as you took your first mouthful, you bit your tongue so blood from the waiter entered through a cut in your mouth, possibly there would be the smallest chance that you could become infected. But it is just as silly as saying you should never travel in a bus in case you crash.

'They say you can't get the AIDS virus from kissing, but I heard it was in saliva and someone got infected from a bite.'

You are both right. The virus that causes AIDS can be found in any body fluid from someone who is infected. It is not always there, and sometimes it is only present in very small amounts. If it is present in saliva, then why don't people get infected from kissing?

The truthful answer is that we don't really know, but this is what we think: for a start it appears that there may be certain things in saliva which attack the virus. Secondly, the virus is often only present in saliva in very small amounts. Thirdly, even if virus from someone infected does enter your mouth it is doomed unless it can find a way into your bloodstream very quickly. In a few seconds a water fall of saliva will flood it out of your cavernous mouth down a huge pipe into an enormous lake of dead burning acid (your stomach), where the virus will instantly be destroyed and broken up into thousands of pieces to be digested. If it survives in a damaged form without being broken up completely, in a few hours it will be ejected from the other end of the gut and down the toilet.

The only way virus in your mouth could infect you is if there was a wound, a mouth ulcer, or a bleeding gum inside your mouth. Doctors have been looking hard at every single known case of infection to find out how it happened. In all the cases so far throughout the world we have not so far as I know found one that has been caught from a kiss.

However, it is possible that a human bite from someone infected can infect someone else. I can think of two cases where this has happened. In the first, a boy is thought to have bitten his brother, and in the second, a girl bit her sister. It is easy to understand why this is different from kissing. After all, the teeth broke through the skin, injecting a small amount of saliva — just as effectively as a snake bite.

'So should I stop kissing my boyfriend?'

Of course not! Although, it is true, if I am completely honest, that if I was young and single and I found out that a girl I was going out with was infected, I probably would not want to give her massive long French kisses!

'Can babies be infected from a mother's milk?'

Yes. HIV can infect a baby, because the lining of the mouth and stomach are so thin that the virus is able to cross. A mother with HIV may be safest not to breastfeed her child. However it all depends. The child is better off with his or her mother's infected milk than being fed on powdered milk made in unsterile ways — milk feed made up with unboiled water can kill babies with diarrhoea and vomiting.

'Can you get AIDS from a toilet-seat?'

No!

'You say that the virus cannot cross the skin unless there is a wound. but if that is true, how does it pass from a woman to a man, or the other way round?'

This is another area where, if I am honest, I have to say we don't really know. The skin on the penis of a man, and inside a woman, is certainly sensitive, thin and delicate. It seems likely that many totally painless, harmless, minute cracks appear in the skin of both partners when they make love. These are how the virus enters. As we have seen, any other sex diseases will make the skin much more likely to bleed

'Can God heal someone with AIDS?'

Yes! God is God and does what he wills. He is the giver of life and the Great Healer. He is just as likely to heal someone of AIDS as he is of cancer or anything else. No one understands why God choses to heal one and not another. He heals far fewer than we who pray would wish. I have heard many reports of people being healed with HIV or AIDS, usually in the poorest nations where it seems the experience of the supernatural is often most developed, but no one I know personally has been healed. However a countless number of people with HIV illness have reported improved general health and well-being following prayer even though they have continued to test HIV positive.

It is easy to pray for healing out of fear rather than with faith. We sometimes pray for healing because we feel mistakenly that it is a bad thing for someone to die. But the bible teaches us that for the believer death is not the end. There is no disaster in death for a follower of Jesus but only hope of eternal life. St Paul said that for him to live was Christ but to die was his gain. So when we pray for healing we also pray that God's will be done. Paul's thorn in his side was not healed. Timothy went on having problems with his digestion. And Jesus himself was allowed by his father to be crucified for our sake just as God allows people to be martyred for the sake of the Gospel today.

'If the virus comes out in urine will our rivers and water supply become contaminated?'

The danger is from germs which live in sewage and cause diarrhoea, not from HIV.

'I have heard that mosquitoes have spread AIDS in Africa. Is this true and could I get AIDS from being bitten in this country?'

Millions of people all over the world are worried about this question, and whenever I am in Africa it is one of the commonest things I am asked about. We are sure that the answer is 'no' in Africa and 'no' anywhere else. If AIDS was being spread by this route, then all the areas of Africa worst affected by malaria would be worst affected by AIDS too, because malaria is carried by the mosquito.

We would also see that all the different age groups were developing AIDS. All ages, after all, get bitten by mosquitoes. In fact, only young children from their mothers and sexually-active young people, in the main, have been affected by AIDS, so we are sure that mosquitoes are not the cause. There may be a small connection between AIDS and malaria, but that is because if you are ill from one thing already, then when AIDS strikes, you are hit twice as hard.

The only insect that we think could possibly transmit HIV is the bed bug, because when they grow big and fat they eat and carry a lot of blood, and some of this can be injected into the next victim. However, the amount of blood is still so small that someone has calculated that you would have to be bitten an average of 15,000 times to be infected!

'Can I get HIV from a barber's blade when shaving me?'

The blade of a barber can transmit HIV if blood is drawn from one person and then the same blade cuts another. You cannot disinfect the blade just by washing. You have to use bleach or other strong disinfectants or heat to a very high temperature.

'How accurate is the HIV test?'

There are many different methods of testing, almost all of which are indirect, looking for antibodies which form as a reaction to the virus. It can take up to 6 months for the antibodies to develop after someone has been infected so someone who takes a risk in January can go on testing negative until July in some cases even though they are infectious. In most cases the most advanced testing systems detect infection around 6 weeks after infection, sometimes earlier. Occasionally the test result can be wrong, and this happens more often with instant testing kits. The testing processes can be complex, and results are sometimes difficult to interpret, and can sometimes be confused by other illnesses. These are all reasons why doctors in many countries like to do two tests, just to make sure, a few weeks apart, using two different methods. There are direct tests for the virus of various kinds but these are very expensive and difficult to do.

'My baby has tested positive for HIV – is he infected?'

Firstly any test can be incorrect in a small number of cases which is why doctors usually like to repeat it just to make sure. Secondly when a baby is born the test does not work correctly. The test we use is for antibodies — which are the body reaction to HIV. But a newborn baby is carrying antibodies from the mother so all babies of an HIV infected mother will test positive for HIV, whether or not they are actually infected themselves. You have to wait for the mother's antibodies to be used up and for the baby to have time to make its own. Around a year after birth the baby can be tested again. In most cases it will test negative, and if the mother was treated with anti-HIV medication during pregnancy then the risk of a positive test a year after birth will be even less.

In 90% of cases the baby is not infected before labour begins. Most infection from mother to child occurs during birth itself. The sicker the mother during pregnancy, the higher her virus levels and the more likely her baby will get infected. Without treatment, around one in four babies will be infected after birth, but this can be as low as 8 in 100 when drugs like AZT (Zidovudine) or HIV protease inhibitors are given to the mother from around 14 weeks of pregnancy until birth and to the infant for 6 weeks afterwards. When drugs are used and the baby is delivered by Caesarean section, the infection rates can be as low as one baby in 50.

'I have heard some say HIV does not cause AIDS'

In a free world of 6 billion people you will always find a small number with very strange ideas on any issue and AIDS is no different. Despite overwhelming scientific research over twenty years, there are a very small number of doctors, scientists and journalists who say things like: "There's no proof HIV causes AIDS." This is a very stupid and dangerous comment. They get publicity because the media like people with extreme views — they make news. The trouble is that they don't understand medical science. You see, nor is there any "proof" in the way they want, that smoking causes lung cancer, yet the evidence is strong enough to convict in a court of law. I say again. You cannot prove that smoking causes cancer. However almost everyone believes this to be a fact, as indeed do I, based on the research. For example we see tobacco tar causes cancer changes in cells in the laboratory. We see smokers are far more likely to get lung cancer than non-smokers. But I cannot prove that the reason a particular person is dying of lung cancer is because they smoked. And smoking itself does not kill: it is the effects of smoking on the tissues of the body that create diseases which then go on to kill.

The smoking argument also applies to HIV. We see the effects of HIV on cells in the laboratory, killing white cells. We know why people get illnesses like TB: it is because these soldier cells are damaged. People do not "die" of HIV any more than people "die" of smoking. They die because of what happens when HIV damages cells in the body. In fact the commonest cause of HIV-related death is TB but I cannot prove to you that the reason someone is dying of TB is because they also have HIV. Some people die of TB anyway and HIV may not be the reason in a particular person even if they are infected. But we do know that people with HIV have a limited life-expectancy compared to those who are uninfected, and can predict the range of problems they will have. Wherever HIV goes, TB usually follows, in a form that is hard to treat and often causes rapid death.

Even a small child understands that a man is given a bottle of infected blood and then a few years later becomes ill. He tests positive for HIV, as does his wife, and their young child. All become ill and all die. Another man given an uninfected bottle of blood is still well twenty years later. He, his wife and child all test negative and remain well, not developing the classic illnesses associated with AIDS.

This is my challenge to people who say HIV does not cause AIDS: if you are so sure, go and inject yourself with blood from someone with HIV. None of them do, because deep down they are still worried. Yet they seem very happy to encourage everyone to ignore health messages, putting people's lives at risk, and as a result even more people may die. I believe this is irresponsible.

In Africa some of these open-air question and answer sessions last several hours with hundreds of people. At the end what I say is this: At the moment people are terrified about all the ways they might get infected without having sex. I do not wish people to be any less terrified of getting AIDS. I just wish they were as terrified of the things they really ought to be terrified about, and not afraid at all of the things which are quite safe. 1 wish people would be as afraid of sleeping around as they are at the moment of actually setting foot inside the home of someone with AIDS.

Almost all the questions I am asked by people concern these same areas of non-sexual spread. I hope you have seen that the vast majority of these risks are very, very small and you do not need to alter what you are doing, whereas now is the time, if you have not already done so, to make some radical changes in your sexual behaviour and expectations and to be very careful about anything which pierces the skin.

Chapter Four

Nowhere to Go

Worse than cancer

It is bad enough being told at the age of twenty-three that you have cancer and are likely to die, but when the disease is AIDS it can seem far worse.

Imagine that you go to the doctor because you have been feeling very run down and tired for the last few weeks. He sends you to the clinic where they do one or two tests. Before you know what is happening they have rushed you up to the ward. They do some more tests and everyone runs around looking very worried.

Then the doctor comes in and tells you that you are very seriously ill and you will need to have a big operation tomorrow. He says you will be in for at least a week. Two days later another doctor comes to see you. He tells you that you have a very rare form of cancer. It is very advanced and the outlook is terrible.

Your whole world has fallen apart in an instant: all your hopes and dreams for the future have been dashed. It cannot really be true. It is hard to take in: your plans for training, a job, a home of your own, maybe to get married and have children, and live to a ripe old age — all of these things have been crushed.

Your parents are beside themselves with worry and grief. What kind of a world is it where children die before their parents? It is like the whole natural order has been turned upside down.

Feeling suicidal

But AIDS can seem worse than any of this. Sometimes I ask a class at school what they would do if they went to give blood and a few days later a letter came asking them to reattend. When they go back a man there tells them that their blood has tested positive for HIV.

Many people tell me they would commit suicide. They could not face the thought of everyone wondering how they had got it. How could they tell Dad? Could they tell him about using drugs, or having been with many women, or being gay and having sex with lots of other boys and men?

Many people do feel like committing suicide and some kill themselves just after finding out about AIDS or an early infection, which is why so much care and support is needed after someone has been told. A friend of mine who is a doctor was shocked one day to wake up in the morning and find that someone had parked his car at the bottom of the garden and had gassed himself with the exhaust. He had discharged himself against advice from the AIDS ward just a few hours previously. He could not face the thought of life with AIDS.

Throw him out

I remember one occasion we had a couple round for dinner. The subject of AIDS came up as it often does. Then the conversation turned to homosexuality and the ways different people develop as they grow up. I was shocked when the wife told us in no uncertain terms that if their five-year-old son was ever to develop signs of being homosexually inclined as a teenager, whether he remained celibate or not, she would throw him out of the house and have nothing more to do with him. No wonder many people with AIDS are careful whom they tell. In most people's minds, to admit you have AIDS is the same thing as admitting you are a loose character with low moral standards, although as we have seen this is often quite untrue.

In fact most women with HIV in some African countries have been faithful before marriage and celibate since, but infected because their partners have not kept themselves in the same way. In India 90% of HIV infected women have had only one partner throughout their lives — their husband.

Collecting the corpse

I went onto an AIDS ward one day and was disturbed to see an anxious young man who was obviously near to death, and dying on his own. I asked where his family were and whether they had been contacted. The answer was that he had been unable to bring himself to tell them what was happening and he did not want anyone else to do so. He was deteriorating fast. Possibly in the morning the ward would contact his mother many miles away, to come and collect the corpse of her son whom she thought was fit and well.

When she came she would probably hardly recognise him. His body was a mere skeleton compared to how he had been seven months ago. His face was sunken and his skin was covered in an angry rash. His body bore the scars of a long hard fight against several infections. He had asked that the death certificate should only say 'pneumonia' because he wanted to save her the pain. If she had known the truth whom would she ever be able to tell?

Living at home

Sometimes the anger is so fierce that it affects those who are doing the caring. A good friend of mine was told by her dad that she was being cut off from the family. From now on it will be as if she did not exist. Her great crime was to fall in love with a man who some years previously had become infected and was now ill. For many months she cared for him, and after he had died, the final crime was to decide to carry on caring for those with AIDS.

A community nurse working for ACET in London had had a long day. That night, in bed with her husband, she began to tell him about someone with AIDS who had been very ill and upset at home, and who she had spent some time with. 'Get out of this bed,' he shouted, 'and don't come back in here until you have stopped going there.'

I do not believe there is a country anywhere in the world where people with HIV have not experienced rejection, hostility, prejudice and fear.

You can begin to understand now why a teacher at a school for young children was upset to find himself on the AIDS ward. Having AIDS was the least of his worries, nor was he afraid of dying. He was scared in case anyone from the school came to see him and it got back to the parents or governors from the staff what was wrong with him. His whole reputation and career would be in tatters.

You can also understand a priest who was constantly afraid that one of his own parishioners that worked in the hospital would come to the ward and recognise him. An increasing number of church leaders are becoming ill from AIDS. We should expect it. If many people are finding faith in Christ, and if HIV survives conversion unless there is a miracle, then we should find many in the church who later become ill although they have been Christians for many years and have been celibate or faithful since finding faith.

Getting the sack

People often lose their jobs when the boss finds out why they are ill.

A number of companies were asked what they would do if they found they were employing someone who had AIDS. Quite a few said they would sack the person straight away. Others said they would encourage the person to leave. Either way it was clear that in the future a lot of people with AIDS in some countries are going to find themselves with no job, even though they may be perfectly well enough to work most of the time.

It is not just businesses that are severe. A solicitor was asked the other day to pack his case and go: 'We don't want that sort of thing here.'

Bust and dying

Every day the number of people with financial difficulties because of AIDS is growing. It frequently happens that a landlord objects if he discovers one of his tenants has AIDS. Maybe he is afraid the rest will move out when they get to hear, or maybe have harsh feelings like some of the others we have seen. Either way, it is quite common for someone to come out of hospital after just being told they have AIDS to discover their belongings have been thrown out and the locks have been changed.

Sometimes the culprit is the person they have been living with. I know of one occasion where someone found the locks changed by a former lover, another where the former lover had cleaned the home out leaving nothing, not even a chair, a lamp, a table or a bed to sleep on. We were able to buy this man a new bed immediately, but a whole home takes time to rebuild.

Wandering the streets

The number of people who have become homeless or destitute because of AIDS is growing each week and is becoming a major problem in some countries.

Whom can I trust?

In all of this you can see that someone with AIDS has most of the things to cope with that someone with cancer has, as well as the extra tragedy of having a terminal disease so young — I speak as a doctor with experience of both diseases. But the worst thing by far is the response of the people around you. Will the next person I meet feel sorry for me (which I hate) or want to see me dead and tell me it's all my own fault? Who is my friend and who is my enemy? If I tell my friend about my illness, will it be kept a secret, or how many days will it take until my friend has told someone else?

No wonder suicide is seen as a better option. The accumulated shock, grief and anguish of losing many relatives and friends can mean that people run out of energy and inner resources.

Chapter Five

What Do You Think?

1. Whose fault is it?

I want now to look at sex and AIDS, and some ways people think about them. Everyone seems to want to point the finger when it comes to AIDS. They begin arguing perhaps about where AIDS first came from. The true answer is no one knows, although we are sure that HIV was around in several parts of the world in the 1960s similar to common viruses in animals and has probably been around in some shape or form for centuries. Because many scientists think it could originally have come from animals in Africa, people immediately think Africa is in some way to blame. This is stupid. Whatever the facts show in the future the disease had to start somewhere and it is no fault where it first came from.

'They should have known better'

The other big area where people seem to point fingers is where particular groups or individuals are infected. Some people say it is their own fault. Depending on how far they take it, you get the impression that some actually believe that anyone who has a certain lifestyle deserves an automatic death sentence.

Some people say those infected should have known better, but they forget that many of those dying now, especially in the poorest nations, were infected before many people had even heard of AIDS, let alone understood how it was spread.

Some people say that anyone, say, with a gay lifestyle or a drug habit should realise that these are wrong and should expect the consequences. This can make those infected feel even more guilty and blame themselves too. They also can often feel very guilty about people they may have infected without realising.

Pointing the finger is the easy way out

Many illnesses are caused by lifestyles that some would question: should we have any sympathy for a man who has smoked fifty cigarettes a day for the last forty years and now has terrible breathlessnes or lung cancer? What about a young girl who falls and breaks her leg at a party because she has had too much to drink?

At the end of the day it is easier to blame people and have nothing to do with them. It is a neat and tidy way of making it someone else's problem. You don't have to feel guilty about not getting involved because in your own mind you have made someone else guilty. It is the same mentality as the man who says you should not help the starving because it is all their own fault for having such large families (even though this is rubbish because the world has the capacity to produce more than enough food for several billion more people).

Harsh churches

Because I have been a church leader as well as having

looked after many people with AIDS, people often ask what I think about AIDS as a Christian. People say different things. Some people say AIDS is the judgement of God on all homosexuals and on heterosexuals with multiple partners. Others have a different view. Some leaders have even said that Christian people should have nothing to do with AIDS while others are saying that every Christian should make some sort of response. A lot of opinions but what should we think about it all?

A personal view

AIDS is not the wrath of God and it never was. If it was the judgment of God on people with multiple sex partners, why is it that homosexuals and heterosexuals are affected while lesbians never so? Lesbians (homosexual women) are the only group in our society, other than monks or nuns, in whom AIDS is almost unknown. It is very hard indeed for a lesbian to pass on the infection to another woman she has sex with. God's judgement is remarkably selective if we are to take such a judgemental position. This would mean that God hates sex between two men, next he hates sex between a man and a woman outside marriage, but he doesn't really mind sex between two women. This is clearly absurd. As a friend of mine said recently, if this is a blast of God's anger about homosexual and heterosexual lifestyles from God's shotgun, he has a pretty poor aim! What about tens of thousands of young children infected in Africa as a result of medical treatments? God's wrath on those who are ill and need medical care?

Nothing new

People get very excited over AIDS. They think that AIDS is something quite new, and as strange as a thunderbolt from heaven. They need to talk to some older people with longer memories and read the history books.

As we have seen, AIDS is just another in a long series of diseases which can be spread by sex. These things have been around for centuries, and AIDS may well have been around in some shape or form for hundreds of years.

Was syphilis the wrath of God? It spread as a plague starting several hundred years ago. There was no cure. It made people sterile and caused them to have all kinds of strange illnesses over many years. It attacked the heart, blood vessels, kidneys, liver, and finally rotted the brain. We used to call the final stages 'paralysis of the insane'. Not a nice way to die.

When penicillin was discovered, did God suddenly decide that he didn't mind and was going to allow the plague to stop? If AIDS is the judgement of God then syphilis is too.

The Bible says we can enjoy most things, but too much can be bad for us. That is why getting drunk is described as a bad thing to do. So then, is the plague of people dying from too much drink, from liver failure, just another disease or the wrath of God on them?

As a doctor I know that AIDS is just a disease. It is caused by a virus common in animals, which has been around almost certainly for a long time. Sex is an easy way for a lazy germ to travel and a great number of germs find it convenient to get around this way. When we have a cure for AIDS, there will doubtless be a whole string of new germs that appear on the scene being spread by sex.

So AIDS certainly is not a "gay" plague, and I do not think it was sent by an angel as a thunderbolt from God to shake us all up.

2. Cause and effect

Common sense shows that you get out of life what you put into it, or as Jesus said, 'you reap what you sow.' This is a personal view as a Christian who takes what the Bible says seriously. I don't ask you to agree with it or like what I say, but it is, I think, a common-sense view.

Any doctor knows that the majority of illnesses he or she sees could probably be avoided or reduced if people lived differently. Heart disease is becoming less common in some countries now, because people are more health conscious. They watch their weight and take exercise. Smoking is also on the decline in many nations; just as well since nicotine is one of the most addictive drugs known to science. You get a shot of nicotine every time a cigarette burns and you inhale the greasy smoke. Smoking kills around 120,000 people a year in UK alone.

The whole of health education is showing people cause and effect: if you smoke you damage your lungs. If you drive when you are stoned out of your brains you are likely to drive off the road and kill someone. If you get drunk you have a hangover. If you inject using a bloody needle you can get hepatitis or develop AIDS.

Cause and effect is the most important lesson we have to learn as children. My daughter shut her thumb in a door and had to be taken to hospital. Her thumb was a mess, but it is perfectly healed now. She learnt that you must not put your fingers in the cracks of doors because the door can close and you can get badly hurt. If she doesn't learn she will be a real danger to herself.

Because I love my daughter I will try to save her the pain of having to learn the hard way. If she jumps on top of her sister's top bunk I tell her off, because I am afraid that one day she will lose her balance and fall. She probably won't do it again after falling, but I would rather she didn't fall in the first place. When you were young your parents probably told you a hundred times a day to come away from something, or to put something down. Most of the time your own safety was the issue. Your mother probably then explained to you, for example, that an oven is extremely hot and if you touch it with your fingers you will burn yourself badly.

None of us is very good at listening at first. Usually there are one or two near disasters: 'I told you so. That was naughty. Now when I tell you next time, you do exactly what I say.' And then we learn.

Strange ideas

People have really strange ideas about God sometimes. They think of him as some great tyrant or bully or some distant figure they can't relate to at all. The Bible says that God is a loving Father, a million times better than your human dad. Because he loves us, he looks on us as his children. He cares about each person as if that person is the only person in the whole world.

Because he cares for us that much he wants to help us and to protect us from our own mistakes. But he respects you as a person and he will never dominate your life. He is always there ready and waiting to help you, but you must ask. He will never impose himself. Nor will he ever go away. You can turn your back on him for years, but he is always there ready and waiting with open arms. There is nothing that you can do that can put you outside his love for you, although you can remain distanced from him with consequences both here and in the next life.

I often think about the story Jesus told about the Prodigal Son. He fell out with his dad and wanted to go off to town and do his own thing. He found living on his own was terrible. He had a really hard time. He spent all his money on trying to live it up and then found himself having to work for a pittance in order to get food. He kept wondering if his dad would accept him again.

After a while he was so fed up he reckoned even if his dad wouldn't accept him back as a member of the family he would prefer to go home on any terms – even as a servant. When he was almost home he got nervous but his dad saw him coming from a distance and rushed out to meet him. The son felt ashamed and wouldn't even look up, but his father flung his arms around him and swept him into the house, cancelled all his arrangements and threw a great coming home party, much to the disgust of a certain other member of the family. Jesus told the story to show us that God's love never goes cold or goes away, just because we go too far away from God.

The Bible contains for me a brilliant guide to healthy living. We often see it as full of negative commands — don't do this and don't do that. My children can also see me as very negative if they don't realise that what I say is actually for their benefit and happiness. It would be a strange dad who constantly let his children put their lives at risk without doing something about it. And it would be a strange God who made a world full of people and just let them get on with it, without giving them some help and advice when they were looking for it.

How to wreck your life

God wants you to know how to avoid the pain of your mistakes, and how to live a happy, full and satisfying life. The Bible is full of examples of cause and effect. In fact you could say it is one of the main teachings of the Bible.

The Bible basically says that if you want to wreck your life then a really good way to do it is to wreck your relationships with people — not just any people, but the people you are close to, your closest friends, your partner, or your family.

And if you want to mess up your close relationships

and family completely, then a good way to do it is to have sex with a person or people you are not married to.

If a father wants to guarantee that he has no relationship with his daughter, so much so that maybe she isn't willing to even call him dad any more, then the quickest way to do it is to sexually abuse her, preferably at a young age over a number of years.

How to be lonely and alone in later life

Tens of thousands of thirty-five to forty-five year olds are having a terrible shock. They grew up deciding it was better just to live together. After three or four relationships they have found themselves on their own yet again. Perhaps with children scattered all over the place that they rarely see.

Many women find one day that their chances now of ever settling down and having a family are vanishing fast. Their most fertile years are over and the men that would have made the best husbands and fathers were long ago snapped up.

Men can also suddenly find that the long party over the years has come to an end. They are no longer as attractive and dynamic as they were. They have lots of memories, but no life-long commitment and no real ideas about how to find one, because most of the women who were into such things settled down with other men long ago.

How to wreck your marriage

If a man wants to destroy his marriage completely overnight, then the quickest way to do it is to cheat on his wife by having an affair, say, with her friend. He will probably lose his children and maybe the respect of his other friends at the same time. Those of us who pick up the pieces find it unbelievable that people can't see things which are staring them in the face. They still go on to make stupid   decisions that anyone watching with any sense at all can see will end in disaster.

If as a young person you want to make it likely that your future marriage will fall to bits within a few years, then a really effective way is to try to get to bed with everyone you can while you can. Patterns don't change because of ten   minutes in a registry office or an hour in a church ceremony of commitment.

If you programme your brain and your body to react in a particular way, then it can be really hard suddenly to become the perfect faithful husband or wife.

Sex before marriage means that your partner in marriage is under a lot of pressure: 'Jacky used to be a lot better in bed. She could really get me going,' or, 'Every time we make love I keep thinking how Bill used to hold me ... he used to do it like this.'

I'm glad that the only person I have ever made love to is my wife — someone who has been my best friend since we were fifteen — and we have been happily married for 24 years. I am glad too that we never made love before we got married. For us it was an expression of total commitment to each other. In our culture, right up until the wedding day there was the opportunity to call it off. Many engagements do not result in marriage, and some engagements should never have gone on into what turned out to be very unhappy marriages.

People need to know what makes a happy marriage, and how they can be reasonably sure they are about to marry the right person. Friendship is the best foundation of all, shared interests and shared faith, while the support of family and friends is also important because it makes it easier if the relationship goes through a troubled time – all life-long relationships go through many periods of readjustment, and rediscovery because we all change and our needs change as we get older.

For my wife and me, our whole language of love has been built up with each other. It is ours alone. It is our secret. It is a private place exclusive to us. No one else can intrude into that special place. It is a sign every time we come together of our exclusive commitment and unity.

The Bible says that when a man and a woman come together they become, in a sense, 'one flesh'. Sex is a mystery, not just a sensation.   People with the best sex-lives are usually those who are in exclusive, stable, loving relationships, who spend time together, who invest in the marriage and take themselves seriously as a couple, who really listen to each other and try always to understand things from the other person's point of view. And that includes how to give each other pleasure in physical ways.

3. A good sex life

Sex is more than a physical act. In medicine I am glad that we are at last moving away from looking at people like cars or other machines, where you replace or repair bits. People are people. Whole person medicine is where we recognise that you are more than a kidney stone or an appendix: you have personal needs, feelings, hopes and fears which go to make up what you are and are actually far more important than the illness. Illness is just a nuisance because it is preventing you from being you.

Glossy magazines have pushed sex as some kind of wonder drug or lifestyle accessory. You get the impression that sex every day keeps the problems or the doctor away. If you are not having sex regularly then they lead you to believe you are underdeveloped, frigid, impotent or just plain stupid. But I don't see a high degree of satisfaction and fulfilment. Agony columns in the same magazines are full of people who are obsessed by poor sexual performance and lack of enjoyment that they dare not tell anyone about so they write instead.

Sex is not a performance: it is possibly the deepest kind of communication and expression known to human beings. But like any language, if there is nothing to communicate then it is empty and hollow, dissatisfying and ultimately as meaningless as any other passing sensation.

When I was at college I remember vividly a couple who visited my room. They had slept together a couple of times over the previous weeks - the first for both of them — and had really regretted it. They were not Christians and it was nothing to do with their own morality. They had come to realise that real sex is not instant; that it takes a while for two people to build up their own language of love, to discover how to give each other the greatest pleasure, and that they had wandered into this area far too soon.

I am glad that when I make love to my wife I can tell her that I have never made love to anyone else. She owns my body and I belong to her. There is a real strength in that. And if difficult times come, and they can come in any relationship, albeit not for long, then the barrier to having sex with another woman is enormously greater than if I were just to fall back to an old pattern of 'sleeping around'.

Making sure you are compatible?

People say you should have sex together before you get married to find out whether you are compatible or not. People who say this obviously don't know the first thing about the facts of life! If they did, they would know that there is no such thing as a man too big for a woman or a woman too big for a man!

Unless the man has a penis thicker than a baby's head the woman will be able to accommodate him. After all, where a man goes in a baby has to come out! Boys are often obsessed with the size of their equipment. Too small or too big? When a woman is aroused, all the parts inside and outside begin to change shape so that even if a man is not particularly well endowed, he will have a snug fit. We have been well designed! It's not what you have but what you do with it that counts.

Incredibly rarely a doctor may see a couple who are unable to have sex because of a slight abnormality; for example, a thin layer of skin completely closing off the woman just inside her. Such a woman does not produce blood when she menstruates, so the reason is usually clear and easily dealt with. But apart from rarities like that, incompatibility does not exist. Impotence in a man can be very distressing, and is far more common than people realise, affecting many men when under pressure, tired or ill. The biggest cause by far is nerves about whether he will perform all right or not, and a man is much more likely to be afraid if he feels he is on some kind of premarriage trial. Marriage gives a couple time, space and security in which to relax.

Secret of a good sex life

However, there is no such thing as an instantly compatible couple. Every person is different and every couple is totally unique. Things that one person may find very pleasurable, another may find a complete turn-off. Good love-making takes time, privacy, care, understanding and good communication. Maybe that is why many couples find their love-making gets better and better as they learn more and more about each other. The most basic requirement, however, is a good warm relationship where, especially for the woman, both partners can really give of themselves in an atmosphere of total security. Only when you are totally secure are you fully free.

When you split sex from the whole-person experience, you are doomed to only part fulfilment. This leads to a steadily worsening spiral, looking always for the ultimate in sexual release. The next person, or this new way of doing it, may yet be better than before. Of course dangerous sex can have an exciting dimension, and that can be the attraction of an affair, but there are plenty of other ways to inject excitement into a stable relationship than being unfaithful, for example making love in what for you both is an unusual location.

How to wreck good sex

In most countries, girls usually realise these things long before the men they go out with do. Most girls need no persuading about the advantages of being in a secure loving relationship. In fact one of the main reasons why (against their better judgement) some are willing finally to sleep with boyfriends is the hope that through offering them sex they will be able to attract their boyfriends into a long term relationship.

Unfortunately in my experience it usually works the other way. A girl a man used to respect, almost revere, he now despises as cheap and worthless, like all the rest. One of a woman's greatest assets in winning a man is her mystery, and the moment she has sex with her boyfriend she is in danger of losing it. The Bible says that when a man has slept with a woman, he 'knows' her. There is a sense in which everything has been uncovered.

4. Sex and the church

Confusion in the church

God saw that all He created was good, including sex: it's the waste of sex outside marriage that causes him grief.

There is confusion in some parts of the church over just about everything at the moment. It seems in some countries you can have a bishop who rejects Jesus as the Son of God, rejects the Virgin birth, thinks that the resurrection never really happened and that the bible is not really to be believed. Once you have a group of people who have decided to reject major parts of the bible, along with many of the historic teachings the church, you have major problems. After all, man's opinion is then as valid as anyone else's. You can end up with as many different religions as there are people.

As an atheist friend of mine said recently, if you want to join the club you must reckon to obey the rules. The trouble here is that it seems some people think they can rewrite the basis of the club's existence, and therefore regard rules they don't like as invalid, and ignore them.

You might forgive existing club members for thinking that these 'radicals' are not radical at all. They have just invented a brand new club of their own.

Daring to be honest

If I am going to be honest and read the bible care fully to understand what the whole of it says about life, not just a sentence or two, then I am going to have to be very careful. You can easily read bits of phrases here and there and string them out to mean whatever you want them to. The overall meaning is vitally important.

Here is my own conclusion about what the bible says about sex and sexuality. You need to read the bible for yourself. I read the entire bible through three times in as many years, often making detailed notes and using reference books to make sure I really understood what was being said. What I am going to say now is in the light of those readings.

At I see it, the bible teaches right from the start that God made man and woman in his own image. His intention is that a man should marry a woman, and that sex is to be a wonderful gift, a mystery uniting a man and woman who have committed themselves to each other in this way for life.

Out of that kaleidoscope of rich physical love are to come children who grow up in a secure loving family, with grannies and grandpas, aunts and uncles, nephews and nieces, and single people included in family life if they want.

Marriage is the basic foundation stone of society. Therefore it is no surprise to the Christian to find that where marriages break down, where there is violence in the home, where spouses cheat each other and stop caring, that children often grow up with deep scars, insecure and unsure of themselves. A lot of vandalism, alcohol problems, drug problems and other situations can be traced to unhappy homes of the young people concerned.

The bible, by encouraging everything that supports a good stable marriage speaks out against anything that undermines marriage as the rock on which society is built. In many Western countries marriage is often regarded as an irrelevance. Marriage is not chic. Look at the adverts. How many women of whatever age, especially in shots of couples, are wearing a wedding ring — or even an engagement ring?

Careers have encouraged women to put off having children for ten years or more. The tragedy is, when they finally want them they often find the peak of fertility has passed, getting pregnant is difficult and the risks of having a baby with an abnormality are increased. In medicine, anyone having a first child over the age of thirty is regarded as an elderly mum because doctors recognise that the female body was not really designed for such a late first pregnancy.

Sex designed for marriage

Because the bible is for marriage, and against anything that discourages marriage, the bible is for keeping sexual union as the exclusive activity of those who are married Before the pill some twenty years ago, sex meant a risk that babies would be born, and babies need Mum and Dad permanently. Any family doctor will tell you that casual relationships are bad for children and bad for family life. Jesus made it absolutely clear that he agreed with the established teaching, which was that sex outside marriage was wrong. In fact he went further to say that even to have a fantasy about sex outside marriage was also wrong.

I am not asking you to agree with this. All I am asking you to do is to be honest with yourself and at least admit that this is what the bible says. It is the teaching that has always been given by the church, although there have always been small numbers of people who have written their own rulebooks, and in the process found themselves outside the church as a result. This teaching is not the teaching of one denomination, but of the whole of the church since the time of Jesus, whether Catholic, Eastern Orthodox, Anglican, Methodist, or whatever. In fact it is one of the few things about which Christians over the centuries have always united.

Stretching the limits

Some people have tried to make out there is a special case for those who have attraction to others of the same sex. The bible teaches that people can be sex aroused in a great number of different situation. It is very explicit. The bible describes men having sex with men, adults having sex with children, men having sex with their mothers, people having sex with animals, orgies, prostitution and many other things. Homosexual sex is mentioned directly in a number of places in the Bible — always as something beyond what is allowed.

However, the Bible also describes very close, warm, intense, loving relationships between people of the same sex — Ruth and Naomi or David and Jonathan for example. David and Jonathan could share as much of lives together as they liked, but they could not indulge in same-sex activity.

Fashionable faith

People say it is very unfair. It is also hard for a woman who finds that the only man she has ever loved is married to another, or for someone who has decided that if there is no one suitable to marry within the community of followers of Jesus then they will remain single. It is also hard for someone when there seems to be lots of potential partners around but none they could face being married to or would trust as father or mother to their children (a good test).

We think in this sex-dominated age that for a man not to express his sexuality by having sex with another person is somehow against the laws of nature and is wrong. It is no different than for a woman to do so, except that a younger man's urges are often far stronger than in a younger woman, a situation which is often reversed in middle life.

Christian faith does not change every time fashion changes, and Christian tradition has always given high honour to those who are celibate. Jesus himself is our example and the Apostle Paul. The time of the early Church was also a culture obsessed with sexual fulfilment and immorality and both Jesus and Paul spoke out clearly in favour of temperance, discipline, self-control, celibacy and faithfulness as part of God's purpose for us all. In the next century people will look with some amusement at the first and second generation who grew up with the pill, the obsession with sex, and the domination of sex diseases.

Sadly they will also record the devastation of family break upon hundreds of millions of children.

5. Caring is not the same as agreeing

You may not agree. I am not asking you to agree, but only to see what I have written is a view which is as valid as yours, and it is the one that reflects the consistent pattern of teaching of the church over two thousand years, whether Catholic, Eastern Orthodox or Protestant.

Practical care

Someone once said to me she was shocked that Christians were involved in compassionate, unconditional care for people with AIDS, because she knew that we disapproved of many of the lifestyles that had caused people to become infected.

I told her she had confused agreeing with caring. They have never been the same thing in medicine. If, as a doctor, I only looked after people who voted for the same party, who held the same faith, who worshipped in the same kind of church, who never did anything I personally could not approve of, I think I should be struck off the medical register right away. Doctors and nurses are expected to give good compassionate care to all who need it and for all illnesses, regardless of how people come to be ill. The same is true for all those involved in the so-called caring professions.

And the fact is that worldwide the churches are at the very forefront of AIDS care and prevention.

Chapter Six

Where Are You Going?

If we are going to look after people who are dying then we need to have come to terms ourselves with what we think about death.

Shaken by the violence

It takes a lot of courage to look death in the eye and keep on looking. The first time it happened to me I was still at school. I was walking along a busy road and saw a bus collide with a woman. She was smashed to the ground instantly. There she was lying on the road bleeding, gasping for breath. We all gathered round. I had never done First Aid at school and didn't know what to do. Someone was holding her head. The driver had got out of his cab shocked, and someone had called for an ambulance. As I watched from a distance she suddenly vomited, choked, went rapidly blue and died.

I went home shaken at the violence of what had happened. You can see 100 things like that on the television but when you see it close up it becomes real. What shocked me even more was to discover afterwards that she had died because she was lying on her back and had drowned in her own vomit.

My second experience of death was after I had just left school. It was a dark wet night and I was sitting on the bottom deck at the front of a big bus with an open rear doorway. As it sped along the black greasy road, I was surrounded by the crash of loose change on the deck. I turned round and saw nothing, and then to my horror through the back window saw the bus conductor lying on the road. He had slipped, hitting his head on the deck before bouncing out onto the tarmac.

I rushed to the bell and rang it for what seemed an eternity before the heavy bus pulled to a halt. I leapt out and raced back. A queue of cars had already stopped. A nurse got out and gave some assistance but he later died of his massively fractured skull.

Most of us don't like to talk about death. We deny death exists. By the way some people talk, you would think they are immortal. In some countries children are often kept well away from funerals, perhaps because adults are embarrassed to cry in front of them.

It is this fear of death, the fear of the unknown that is the main reason why AIDS is so scary. People often ask me how I could spend so much time with people who are dying - it used to be cancer, then it was AIDS. The answer was because I know where I'm going.

When I had just qualified as a doctor, one of the first patients I had was a retired woman who was dying of cancer. I remember sitting on her bed one afternoon and she took my hand. 'You'll remember me when I've gone, won't you,' she said. I nodded and she went on: 'You know where you're going, don't you. You believe?'

I had never said anything to her about faith. I do not carry a label, or a symbol, or a bible, but she had picked something up. She sensed that I was at peace with her dying. She could see that I was not afraid and that I was not going to abandon her because hope of her cure had abandoned me.

It is only as we get older that we get screwed up about dying. Young children are very matter of fact. Children who are dying usually treat it as a part of normal conversation, and are then very suprised to find out that all the adults cannot cope. They quickly learn to shut up so as not to upset their parents and the nursing staff.

I think some of the fears I used to have stemmed from some of the things I had been told such as, 'He would have swallowed his dentures so we take them out' (how anyone could swallow a set of false teeth was beyond me, but it made me think that something violent happened after death). I was also told that after people died it was like the floodgates opened: waterworks and bowels emptied over the bed. You can imagine how relieved I was as a medical student to discover that these things do not happen: when managed properly, death is almost always a peaceful and dignified thing. Often the relative in the room is not even sure if the person has died or not; he or she just appears to be sleeping.

Death is a mystery

If you have ever had the privilege of sitting with someone who is dying at the moment of death, you have experienced a mystery. Here is a woman bounded by place and time. You are sitting there holding her hand. She is breathing quietly. Most of the time she is asleep, but occasionally she opens her eyes or says a word. She is not in any pain, she is not anxious and she knows exactly what is happening. She is not afraid and is at peace.

As you are sitting there you notice that her breathing has become more laboured, and she seems sleepier. Over what seems like hours, but is in fact a few minutes, the breathing changes again. The nurse comes in and says her pulse is very weak and rapid now. There are small beads of sweat on her brow.

Gradually her breathing seems to fade away, and is gone. You wonder if she has died. After a few minutes you get a shock when she suddenly takes another deep breath before all is quiet again. And after a while you realise she has gone.

A dead body is still alive

Nearly all the cells in her body are still alive. Her kidneys will be useful to someone if removed in the next half an hour — so long as she does not have cancer or HIV. Her brain-cells are too damaged to live for long, but her skin will still be alive in a week. The cornea (the clear bit of the eye) if removed by late tomorrow, will give a child sight and her heart may still have cells within it which are beating. Her gut is still contracting and the stomach is still digesting food. All the proteins in her body are still there, the bone marrow is still producing new blood cells. So what has happened?

At the end of the day it is a mystery. I always say that the nearest an atheist ever gets to a profound religious experience is his own death, and death heightens spiritual awareness in every way. It is a brave person who has just watched this mystery, or perhaps watched the birth of a child, who can walk away as convinced as before that there is no God.

Four reactions to dying

When you know you are dying, four things start to happen. The first is that your priorities change. What is the point in carrying on with your College course when the doctors have told you that you will probably be dead by Christmas?

The second thing is it alters your relationships. You find your best friend can't cope and hasn't visited you once in hospital, while someone in the same year whom you never thought much of has been a real support and nothing is ever too much trouble. Sometimes it takes a terminal diagnosis for some people to really work out who they are, and who is important to them.

It can be a time of great regrets and some people find themselves looking back and wondering how they would have done things differently if they had known life was going to be so short.

Finally, people find they are looking forward. Most people I talk to are not so much afraid of death as afraid of dying: they are afraid of becoming incontinent, of losing control, of becoming a burden, of being totally dependent, afraid of pain, afraid of suffocating to death, afraid of losing the ability to think, move or remember.

And then there is another dimension: is there really no more to life than life? Is there really no more to me as a person than the molecules that go to make up my body? When I die, will that be the end, or is there another kind of existence after this one?

Deathbed conversion

These and many other questions often cause people to search. They go to mediums, spiritualists, traditional healers and any other agency that will reassure them that there is in fact life beyond the grave. Deathbed conversion is very common and very real. The thief on the cross turned to Christ in the act of dying. I remember a man with lung cancer who came into St Joseph's Hospital while I was there. He looked at the nuns and said: 'I'm an atheist. Do I have to be Catholic to be here?'

We explained that people of all faiths and none were equally welcome. I don't think anyone asked him about any matter regarding personal faith or beliefs, until some two weeks later he suddenly raised the matter again and asked to see a priest. He had undergone a profound turnaround as he approached the end, without a single word being said.

More to life than life

As a Christian I believe that there is a life after this one, and that death is merely a gateway from a physical world, limited by space and time, to another dimension. Jesus taught quite clearly that when this is all over, each of us will have to give an account of what we have done with our lives.

Jesus also showed us that no none of us are perfect in and of ourselves: none of us can please God. None of us is perfect enough to enter his presence and survive, But the good news is that God has bridged that huge gulf between us and him by sending Jesus. The things that you and I have done wrong have eternal consequences. We're responsible, and the penalty for what we have done is ultimately death and extinction.

But God sent Jesus to receive the punishment that should have been ours. By dying for us, Jesus set us free from the effects of our own wrongdoing. Through Jesus, for those who accept him and receive him, God has chosen to forgive us completely and wipe the record completely clean. Through Jesus we call on the unreachable, unknowable, unfathomable God as our Father.

For those who believe, the moment of death is for us a change from being only partly aware of God and his love, to being fully and completely in his presence, an experience of heaven itself. For someone who never knew God and the things of God, the bible teaches us that life after death will be an unpleasant, uncomfortable disappointment.

This teaching about what happens after death has always been a central part of the church, but immediately raises a question in many people's minds especially when they read that many Churches are becoming involved in providing practical care for people with AIDS. If Christians believe some people may find themselves separated from God after death, then they will surely want to get at every person they meet who is dying and preach the gospel?

I was talking to a prominent member of an AIDS organisation recently who also incidentally has AIDS himself. He is a convert to Buddhism and freely admitted with a smile that when he was with people who had AIDS all he really wanted to do was tell them about his faith, but he knew he could not.

What do you want? If someone with AIDS asks to see a chaplain, he is asking for spiritual help. If all the chaplain is interested in doing is visiting him at home to do cooking, wash clothes, help with the children and bring water, you can imagine he might well feel let down. However, if someone with AIDS has asked for someone to help with the washing and all the person seems to want to do is talk religion, you can imagine the person might well have good cause to feel annoyed.

It is a real privilege to be allowed to be with someone who is approaching the end of his or her life. It is a very special time, as all who have been involved will know. People are rightly very sensitive to others rushing in insensitively to someone who may be too weak to say 'no' or 'please go away. Often it is only afterwards that the upset comes out and the person who is ill pleads for a certain person never to come into their home again. Behind the polite facade there can be real anguish which is often not expressed at the time. If you are vulnerable you think twice before antagonising someone on whom your life could depend.

Helpful or dreadful

If a doctor at a clinic asks a volunteer agency for a community visitor, he expects practical help, not a chaplain. If it gets back that a particular visitor spent all night (it may not be true, but only a tiny part true) trying to convert his patient, the doctor may well feel justifiably angry. As far as he is concerned, the community service is completely useless.

It is not a service to him as a doctor because he would be extremely worried about asking someone else to go in from that group again. It is not a service for the patient because what the patient wanted was good company and a helping hand, and he or she got a preacher!

The doctor comes to the conclusion that the AIDS programme is only interested in serving the local priest by trying to convert people. If that is the case, he as a doctor will campaign to make sure everyone knows about these dreadful people.

Guest and servant

There is a right time and a right place for everything. And it all depends on local culture and custom. For example, in many parts of Uganda the level of church commitment is so strong that it would be very strange for a visitor from a church-based AIDS programme not to offer a prayer at every visit. Indeed if you do not offer to pray it is very likely that you will be asked to do so in any case. Christian prayer in the home is a usual, expected part of that community ministry. Prayer is a way of life. But in Thailand or parts of India the expectations may be very different: And we need to be very sensitive to these things.

It depends so much on the nature of the service you have advertised and that people are referring to. However whatever the culture, however hostile it may be to the Christian faith, the following is always true:

If you are making someone a meal and because he has noticed that you are always there, you never complain, you accept him as a person, you are happy to look after him even though he senses you do not share his views on lifestyle, because of all these things and because he knows you go to church he asks you about your faith, then this is a wonderful time to share a little of the hope that is in you, and perhaps to bring spiritual comfort and peace.

He is driving the conversation, and it would be stupid and unfriendly not to answer his questions. You might find that in the context of his own searchings, he finds it reassuring to have someone around like you who has a faith. You might even find that he asks you to pray for him — it is surprising how often an atheist has faith in the prayers of someone else! But in everything, your attitude must be that of a servant: how can I be of most help today? Also that you are always there as a guest and never to take over. By the way, the Buddhist I mentioned earlier eventually found faith in Christ in just such a way.

Schools education

The same principles apply in schools education. Schools work is a very sensitive area where everyone may have strong views on how sex education and AIDS should be taught. And again this will vary between countries, areas, communities and schools. People can be afraid that activists will try to use the AIDS crisis to promote inappropriate condom use in schools or to promote extreme moral views and attitudes.

A schools' educator is there at the invitation of the teacher to be a servant to the school, as a guest in the classroom. Topics to be covered, methods and general approach should all be agreed beforehand.

Working in schools is a privilege and should not be a platform for promotion of personal beliefs, without the approval of those whose guest you are. However, if in the context of religious or life skill classes an educator is asked by teacher or pupil to present a personal perspective for example on the Christian hope of life after death or view of sexuality, then that is a different matter, so long as it is presented as a personal view open to discussion and debate. But as I say, be guided in all things by the local school and the teachers within it. They will often give you far greater freedom than you might have imagined.

In summary then, AIDS is a terrible disease that kills a great number of people, spread by a virus through sharing needles or sex with infected people. It hits us in two areas where we feel most vulnerable: our morality and our mortality, and makes us question what we do and what we are.

Now is the time for action.

Time for Action

The first thing you may need to do is sort your own life out. I find it depressing to see how many people or older people only really work out the meaning of their lives when their lives are almost at an end. Will it take a terminal diagnosis for you before you put your own house in order? Urgent decisions may need to be made today to change your sex life or injecting drugs, as well as to work out what is important to you.

What is important to you?

What will really make you happy in the long-term? Who are your most important relationships? I don't just mean this year, but over the next few years in the future. Do you know who your real friends are and to whom you belong?

These are important questions. Many people say after becoming Christians: 'If only I had known then what I

know now, my life would never have been such a mess.'
The   tragedy is that it often takes a terminal diagnosis, or
a near fatal accident, to bring someone to a full stop for
long enough to think and feel straight. Most people you
know are probably happy enough at the moment to hurtle
through life from one relationship to another, from job to
job, no long-term plan in mind, just living for another day.

But people living like that often find themselves washed
up on a beach. A woman discovers at thirty-eight that the
man she has been living with and promised her marriage
and children has been cheating with another woman for
the past two years and is leaving her. A man finds he has
achieved the dream of his business, but at the cost of losing
his wife and children. He discovers too late that money
buys lots of attention but no friends. Another man discovers
after a string of relationships that he is   disillusioned and
is not sure what love is any more.

Living life to the full

You are important. I believe you were made for a
purpose and that you will find your greatest happiness
finding that purpose for yourself. Part of that involves
starting to live for others. Jesus said that the only way you
will find your true self, that is becoming truly human, is by
losing yourself — not by becoming a passive doormat that
everyone else can tread on, but by letting go of the right to
run your life your own way, and instead inviting Jesus to
show you how to live his life. I believe God has a plan for
you and that because he loves you, his plan is the one that
will make you truly happy.

The most important part of that plan is that he wants
you to know him personally, as your friend, and that he
wants you to have new power, strength and inner resources
so that you can live life to the full. This brings wholeness
and sometimes physical healing as well.

Getting involved

Secondly, there is some action you can take that will be of practical help to those who have AIDS. You might want to become a volunteer, to offer, to visit someone who is ill, or to help support their family. Or you might want to help save lives by telling people how to protect themselves against HIV. Why not talk to others in your church, or to other people involved already in a Christian response to AIDS, and offer time to them. You will find many resources to help you on the ACET International Alliance website. You can download them and print them out.

What can be done?

Start with what you have. I recently visited a school for AIDS orphans and an income generation project started by six grandmothers in a very poor area of Uganda. They started with what they had and got on with it themselves, gradually mobilising others in the village and little by little the work has been established. They saved up and bought some land. Then they saved to buy a cow. The milk from that cow pays to run the school. Gradually they made bricks and replaced the straw roof on poles with a small building. And then they built another. They started to teach the children as best they could in their own spare time. Everyone was helping. Some brought food, others cooked, others carried water each day so the thirsty children could drink. The grandmothers realised they needed some training and went off to government programmes to get a basic qualification. A visitor came and gave them money to get electricity. Another provided a pipe for running water. Another gave them a sewing machine to train older girls… and gradually the work has grown.

Every church can encourage members to do something to help. As George Hoffman, the founder of

Tear Fund, once said: "You can't change the whole world but you can change someone's world somewhere."

Go and save someone's life today.

Go with food to a family stricken by AIDS today.

Go and comfort a widow or an orphan today.

Go and encourage someone who is giving their lives to AIDS ministry today.

Pray for God's protection on them and for God's provision.

And you may be part of the answer to those prayers !

Practical help for yourself

Thirdly, you may want to talk to someone about some of the matters raised in this book. For example you may be worried that you are infected or someone you know may be. You may need to talk with your pastor, or to your doctor to get the expert advice that you need.

Things you can do for those affected by HIV

1. Take them to the hospital if they are sick.

2. Visit them at the hospital, care centre or in the community itself.

3. Give tuition to their children.

4. Help get admission for their children into school.

5. Help them gain employment.

6. Pray for them.

7. Welcome them to your church and accept them as part of your community.

Chapter Seven

What Can We Do?
Time for Action

Good Practice in HIV/AIDS Projects
by Mark Forshaw — Africa Inland Mission

What can we do? How can you and I make a difference? Firstly, always start with what you already have. It's a scriptural principle. God's work done in God's way never lacks God's supplies, as Hudson Taylor, the famous missionary to China once said. So what is God calling *you* to do? What has he laid on your heart?

You need neither funds nor a large team to start. It costs nothing to care for a friend or neighbour, nor to talk to your own children and colleagues about HIV and AIDS, nor to include HIV issues in your church teaching programme, or work training schemes, or school curriculum. Together we can make a real difference.

You may not be able to save the whole world but you can save someone getting HIV somewhere. You may not be able to help all those with HIV or orphaned by it, but you can give practical help and encouragement to a few, and you can get involved in other projects that are already running. But do it all in fellowship with others. Such work can be stressful, draining and lonely and you will need people supporting you too.

What about larger projects? Thousands of programmes have been developed, countless papers published and   millions of dollars expended in the struggle against HIV/AIDS. Yet spread of the pandemic rapidly continues. Many governments and NGO agencies now recognise that their strategies are failing to stem the tide, yet continue to pump money into condom distribution alone and one-off awareness campaigns, neither of which address related problems such as poverty, education, the rights of women, and broader lifestyle questions.

Here are some stories to encourage you: remember these are lessons from different countries which need careful adaptation to your own situation. However the Case Studies illustrate many general points which are vitally important.

Every one of these stories has a small beginning. An individual touched by the love of God, and deeply affected by what AIDS is doing to the world He made. People who felt they *had* to do something, and who began, usually with almost nothing, step by step, following God's calling, in fellowship with others and learning from those around them as they went. In many cases the road was long because there were few role models for such programmes at the time. But now the programmes they began are an inspiration and practical encouragement to us, and accelerate us on our own journeys.

Case Studies from India

J is about 19 years old and comes originally from Kolkata. Her mother was a CSW who died of AIDS. The family moved to Mumbai where her mother plied her trade and J cared for the brothel keeper's kids and also worked as a maid. The family shuttled frequently between Mumbai and Surat.

At the age of 12 J fell in love with a 30 year old man because he used to take care of her. He took her to the railway station, applied sindur, put a mala around her neck and said they were married, even though she had not yet reached menarche. He used to force her to have sex and she would scream. She finally reached menarche at the age of 13, ran away back to her mother and again worked as a maid for the brothel keeper's children. The brothel keeper tried to persuade J to marry her son to pay off her mother's loan, but she was not ready for another traumatic marriage. The brothel keeper insisted that her mother had borrowed Rs.10,000 and J was forced into the CSW work and was paid nothing for a year. From Surat she went back to Mumbai to another brothel and then shuttled between brothels for the next 2-3 years.

Finally the police rescued her and sent her to a rehabilitation home from where she was sent to an Auntie to be cared for. She fought with the Auntie and went back to her husband for 8 months and then went back to the rescue home. She was taken to another brothel where she developed TB and took partial treatment only. From here she was rescued by a Social Organization in Bombay and taken to a Care Centre for treatment since a blood test has revealed that she is HIV infected. She is being started on anti TB treatment and will be transferred to a women's rehabilitation home.

B is a 25-year-old Punjabi whose husband was a truck driver who drove trucks on the Delhi to Punjab to Bombay routes. Her husband died 3 years ago of AIDS. His blood had been tested for HIV previously when he started suffering from continuous fevers, but he kept the HIV+ve blood report in his truck with the truck papers and did not tell his wife. When he became so ill that he could no longer work, he returned to his home in Punjab and he expired there in a separate room of his parent's house as no one would touch him.

B had 2 children. The oldest one is a son, 6 years old, and he is not infected with HIV. When B was pregnant for the second time, she went for ANC because she developed some genital ulcers and her blood tested HIV+ve. Because of her HIV+ve status she could not find any hospital in Delhi where she could have her baby delivered. She was taken to Punjab and put in a separate room of a small hospital used by fisherfolk where her baby daughter was delivered by a traditional birth attendant (dhai). This child was HIV infected and died at 2.5 years of age.

B's in-laws blamed her for the death of her husband and her daughter. She had heard that whoever had HIV/AIDS was given an injection to kill them. Thus it was that when a Social Organization went to search her out to give some support for her son's education, B spoke to them and requested the injection so that her wretched life would be ended.

B was treated at a Care Centre for TB and she is presently living with her parents and works in a factory for about Rs.1800 per month. Her mother helps her a lot as does her sister, but her father, a helper on the trucks, drinks a lot and beats her and others. The Social Organization gives some support to her son and so far her CD4 count is OK.

C was living in a small hut near the railway track in one of the slums in a metro city in India. Her husband had died a few months earlier with AIDS. She had no job and was displaced from her parents in Bihar. She was found to be HIV+ at the time of her husband's death. She had three daughters (aged 6, 4 and 2 years) to look after. The eldest daughter couldn't be sent to school. We felt appalled at the situation she was in.

She has a job in a small-scale industry. Two children are going to school, she is on ART and she is able to manage financially. We realized how our few words of encouragement, regular visits by social workers, neighbours, industry owner and treatment at the care centre all contributed to her being able to stand on her feet once again, and finding hope in the fact that God cares!

Care Case Study — FACT Zimbabwe

In the face of a high level of need and limited formal health resources, Dr Geoff Foster a paediatric doctor in Zimbabwe founded FACT (Family AIDS Caring Trust) in Mutare, Zimbabwe, He saw the pressing need to mobilise the local community to provide care. Churches were approached who had individuals willing to be trained to provide help for families and neighbours in their communities. FACT home care programmes are co-ordinated by experienced health workers who are responsible for local teams. Each team is headed by a volunteer, managing other local church volunteers who provide the actual care to those in need in their areas.

The training of volunteers consists of basic counselling and care skills. Care skills required for people ill at home are: bathing and personal hygiene, washing clothes and bed linen, house cleaning, provision of appropriate food and the treatment and dressing of minor wounds. While the main aim of the volunteers is to attend to those infected with HIV, they are trained to care for all who are chronically ill or dying, e.g., people with TB, diabetes or simply from old age. It felt wrong to visit only those who were ill due to HIV while not caring for their neighbours who were equally ill but not necessarily HIV positive.

Above all it is necessary for volunteers to recognise that the needs of those they visit are not purely physical, but also emotional and spiritual. Volunteers are drawn from the local community and it is often their neighbours they are caring for. The formation of serving relationships are the basis for good practical care and supportive counselling.

The majority of those visited are living with members of their families and the role of the volunteers is also to support them. They offer advice on ways to deal with different infections common to HIV; other informal and formal services available and how to access them. Importantly the volunteers also offer emotional and spiritual support to the family carers.

Through this relatively low skill and low cost team a larger number of people are able to receive help, utilising the traditional family and community caring mechanisms. Through volunteers, each church is able to reach into its community to serve and support families, neighbours and other carers. Volunteers contribute to programme development with data collection and in decision making and planning meetings. This is good practice: involve people who are closest to those who need help.

Home care helps those most in need of assistance in their own areas. However providing practical care alone only meets physical needs. There are also very real emotional needs as people face prejudice and rejection, and spiritual needs as they are facing death. Care must therefore encompass counselling of the individual by appropriately trained and supported workers.

For Christian organisations, home care and counselling can be opportunities for finding faith, as people with no human hope discover eternal hope through Christ. Care for a PWA (Person With Aids) is a powerful way of sharing the love of Christ practically within the community and sometimes this can lead to naturally sharing Jesus, our motivation for caring.

Basic physical care of sick people is an obvious need that must be met. Destigmatisation, normalisation and inclusion by family, friends and community are also all needs though less immediately obvious. They can all be achieved by low-cost, yet trained and caring volunteer home visitors, who are themselves, well supported and managed.

The relational-based care offered by the volunteers naturally opens up opportunities to raise awareness and understanding more widely about HIV/AIDS and especially how it is transmitted and prevented. HIV/AIDS prevention that develops out of the context of care often makes it easier to talk about sensitive social and moral issues People whose friends or family are infected are facing the reality of the disease and therefore tend to listen and subsequently pass on information to others. For an AIDS organisation working in prevention, one of the best entry points is care, which most often also brings credibility to their work

Summary on Care

- Community based care reaches more people.
- PWAs often prefer to be cared for in their own homes.
- Be prepared to care for those with many different illnesses, not only those living with HIV/AIDS.
- Families, friends, communities and volunteers are a resource for care.
- Communities must own the work and so must be consulted from the beginning and throughout the life of the programme.

- Care in the community provides opportunities for prevention education.
- Community based care is most often cheaper than hospital based care.
- Care should be holistic: physical, emotional, social and spiritual.
- Effective care in the community is best linked to other services and works in partnership with them e.g. local hospitals.
- Communities have many resources within them that can be drawn upon.

Summary on use of Volunteers

- Ask the question: is the use of volunteers appropriate, how, where and to what extent?
- Selection criteria must be established at the start. Motivation is key.
- Relevant training at the start and throughout the programme
- Monitoring and support of volunteers throughout the programme life
- Involvement in decision making and planning.
- Clear parameters for volunteers on what is expected of them and when they should refer to paid staff.
- Regular group and individual monitoring and support of volunteers by the organisation. People are our greatest and most precious resource.

Issues in Counselling

- A central part of care and prevention.
- Training is critical.
- So is supervision and clear boundaries i.e. know when to stop and who to pass issues to.

Prevention Case Study — ACET Uganda

The aim in all HIV/AIDS care and prevention work should

be the reduction of the spread of HIV. Here is the greatest challenge to those in HIV-related work: are you spending as much effort and resource on saving lives, as in caring for those affected. You only have today to save someone's life and the next 10 years to plan their care. We must do all we can to fight this terrible problem. Care programmes, while vitally needed, are no answer on their own to the spread of AIDS.

But changing behaviour is a real challenge. HIV/AIDS awareness campaigns and education alone have limited impact in changing high risk activities of individuals. Information received by an individual does not necessarily mean that the individual understands, relates to or wishes to change their behaviour.

ACET Uganda, under the present leadership of David Kabiswa, has developed effective resources now used across Africa and even further a field in India. Like his fellow Ugandan team members, David could not stand by and watch the vulnerable, such as school children, women and street children, become increasingly at risk of infection. Together the ACET Uganda team has developed a three-pronged approach to communication to assist effective and sustainable behaviour change.

A. Information:

People must know the facts. This must be designed to meet individual and local needs. It must be able to fill gaps in information and lay a foundation for understanding the medical, social, economic, cultural and spiritual issues related to HIV/AIDS. But facts alone will rarely change behaviour.

B. Identification:

Assisting individuals to understand high-risk behaviours that they are, or could be, involved in. Help people make important lifestyle choices understanding the options and consequences of particular behavioural practices. This method is in contrast to the "Fear Method" of many HIV/AIDS campaigns.

C. Interaction:

Having been shown the choices, the individual is then encouraged to think through the options. These relate to life-skills that reduce vulnerability to infection, enabling long-term fulfilling relationships, taking personal responsibility for their behaviour, having confidence to make and live by their own decisions, and respecting the worth of others.

As ACET Uganda developed its HIV/AIDS prevention work it soon became apparent that HIV/AIDS could not be dealt with in isolation and it was necessary to deal with general sex education and, importantly, the development of an individual's relationships through developing personal self-worth and a high regard for others. These are skills that are critical not only to HIV/AIDS prevention but also to the general development of every individual.

ACET Uganda describes lifeskills as "formal and informal teaching of requisite skills for survival, living with others and succeeding in a complex society. It can no longer be assumed that these skills are automatically learned or that they are automatically passed on, as was in times past." (Life skills Education for Responsible Behaviour among Adolescents, ACET Uganda) Many existing cultural teachings may not prepare people for new pressures.

For example, with increased urbanisation, people are facing new economic and social pressures, while traditional social structures are breaking down. Development of life skills by people (in particular those most vulnerable, such as young people and women) can equip them to respond more positively to the challenges that they face in life.

How life-skills are learned

ACET Uganda uses interactive teaching methods to provoke people to think and discuss issues that affect them, assisting them to analyse situations they will face and their responses.

Peer pressure is very effective in developing individual thinking and social understanding. This can be both negative and positive. The role of the education team is to develop peer-group thinking that will help reinforce and sustain positive and healthy behaviour.

- Focus group discussions.
- Debates and Panel Discussions.
- Films, reels, slides and video. "Do not expect films to speak for themselves" but they can form the stimulus for good discussions.
- Questionnaires.
- Talks, not long lectures, but short and dealing with contemporary issues.

There are common principles for educators/ facilitators to employ during the learning process:

- The issue is not primarily raising awareness, but assisting personal and community behaviour change.
- Attention to vulnerable groups, in particular women and young people. Research their needs.
- Commitment to people.
- Respect for the listener and their views.
- Co-operative not competitive learning.
- Importance of peer education.
- Interactive methods of learning.
- Time for reflection.
- Clarity of the message.
- Relationship building.
- Training of others to assist in the process e.g. peer educators.

The Gospel — a framework for life

For Christians involved in life skills education the gospel can be brought in naturally when appropriate, for many it offers them a framework for life. It is the news of Jesus Christ who can help people face the challenges of life. It may not always be appropriate to be evangelistic, but often educators are asked where they receive the strength and purpose to face life's challenges and can legitimately testify to their faith.

The integration of HIV/AIDS Prevention with other issues

Addressing HIV/AIDS prevention education should form part of a more comprehensive teaching on lifeskills. The educators of ACET Uganda have gained credibility, in part because they are dealing with many of the other pressures people are facing. For other organisations such as FACT, involvement in the care of people living with HIV/AIDS has given them the basis and opportunity from which to undertake prevention education.

Church Mobilisation Case Study — Chikankata Hospital

A church which serves the community

It is of course important that the church *serves* the local community. But part of serving means handing power and decision making to the community, and even to people living with HIV/AIDS. The central verse in Mark's gospel, Mark 10 verse 45 describes Christ as a servant "For even the Son of Man, did not come to serve, but to serve and to give his life as a ransom for many". Not only a servant, but a servant who gave his life.

The Salvation Army hospital at Chikankata, describe their education work 'community counselling' as "an activity expressed through dialogue, directed towards genuine transfer of responsibility for prevention — from health personnel and other concerned 'helpers' to individuals, families and perhaps most importantly, communities" (AIDS Management An Integrated Approach Campbell I.D, Williams G). Such a community wide interactive approach is essential in the context of AIDS in communities with high rates of HIV infection. The task of prevention is very great and communities must own the desire to change. Instruction alone is not enough. They need education, information and training from people they respect. The church must serve in order to mobilise the community.

The Word of God

The size and moral nature of the epidemic has left many programme implementers uncomfortable with the slow pace at which the church, missions and Christian NGOs have responded. Church leadership is key in the mobilising of HIV/AIDS programmes. If church leadership remains unmotivated or, worse, prejudicial about church involvement, time needs to be invested to help influence a change in this attitude before sustainable action is expected from a church or group.

When you have support and encouragement of the church leadership the resources within the church can easily be mobilised. The key that appears is the power of the Word of God with the Holy Spirit to motivate, to care, and to give people a framework for life. Christian care must model that of Christ, which was not restricted to the physical needs of people, but went way beyond this to their emotional, relational and ultimately spiritual needs. Christians have an opportunity through HIV/ AIDS care and prevention education to practically express the love of Christ for the marginalised, but also for all in the community living under the threat of AIDS.

Mobilising a Church Case Study — TAIP, Jinja, Uganda

Under the leadership of Pastor Sam Mugote a number of the members of Deliverance Church, Jinja, formed a group to offer physical and spiritual care to people in their community living with HIV/AIDS. They were motivated by the many needs of their neighbours but also by the call of God's Word to care sacrificially for those in need, without prejudice or judgement. The programme grew through other churches seeing the positive impact upon the lives of individuals, the community and the church itself, and requesting to become part of the programme or to be allowed to replicate the work. The Deliverance Church formed TAIP, The AIDS Intervention Programme, to enable and assist churches to respond to the HIV/AIDS epidemic in their communities.

The aim of TAIP is to assist churches to develop sustainable support to people living with HIV/AIDS. Churches are facilitated to plan and manage both care and prevention programmes through volunteer-based work to their immediate communities. The foundation for these programmes is a spiritual premise that Christians should take initiatives in the HIV/AIDS epidemic.

The implementers of the care and prevention work are individual volunteers from churches. The majority of them are untrained in formal health care, but have been equipped to provide the basic physical care that people living with HIV/AIDS need in their homes. Furthermore the volunteers are trained to provide counselling intended to meet the emotional needs of both the PWA and their families. They also offer advice on nutritional matters and other services available to individuals and families. At the heart of the provision of this practical care the love of Christ is shared.

Generally, the TAIP team works with churches that approach TAIP for guidance. In the words of Pastor Sam Mugote, he sees the role of TAIP as assisting churches "to develop work that churches are already doing", that they care about people and the biblical model for life. Mugote will and has worked with many churches that fit this description. Such is his deep desire to see the needs of those affected by AIDS that he will help any church respond when he can.

The churches that seek assistance and are selected to receive training share two key qualities. Firstly, they see the need of people in their community infected by HIV and the effect this has on their families and community. Secondly, the church is active in the verbal and practical proclamation of the gospel i.e. has recognised and is already practising a response to the call of God's Word to tell people of the good news of Jesus Christ in word and deed. These are fundamental building blocks, without which it is difficult to then start an HIV/AIDS programme. The role of TAIP is to offer guidance on how a congregation may direct their vision and skills to offer effective care and prevention.

As stated above the experience of TAIP is that a local church must already show evidence of commitment to and practical outworking of, the biblical teaching cited above. From this starting point it will be more of a natural development for churches to then make a local response to the HIV epidemic.

The TAIP team begin by making an initial visit to a church to meet with the minister, church leadership, and interested individual members in the congregation. It is important that the leadership not only agrees to the development of a programme but is also actively involved in the work. The church may meet a number of challenges through which the active support of leadership is needed. Volunteers may face prejudice and will certainly need regular support and understanding when involved with chronically ill people and their deaths. The TAIP team train motivated *and* selected members of the church to become a Support Action Group (SAG) to visit people with HIV/AIDS. This group of volunteers is also equipped to be able to review its activities and support one another by meeting together regularly.

The emphasis of the TAIP training and of the SAG volunteers is to develop relationships with individuals. This meets one of the central needs of people, to realise that they are loved and have worth and it is from this base of emotional support that the other elements of care can be supplied.

It is important to note that the experience of TAIP has been that the mobilisation of a church can take between six and eighteen months as volunteers are selected, trained and learning practically applied between training sessions. Training is then followed up by supervision, support and update training visits by TAIP. Another important factor in the development of the church's programme is clear liaison and communication with the local community. The community should agree to and own the initiative and this will often require time and resources dedicated to developing relationships, even training in the development of surveys and planning with communities.

It is the experience of TAIP and other organisations that volunteer-based projects can be developed with less difficulty in rural areas compared to urban areas. The main reason for this is the availability of volunteers with time to care for people outside of their own families. In urban areas there are often reduced family structures and the need to earn a wage can severely restrict the time volunteers have to offer. A solution has been to mobilise those who do have some available time. Furthermore training has often concentrated on the training of families to provide more of the care needs of people living with HIV/AIDS.

TAIP has seen that a programme developed naturally by one local church provoked other neighbouring churches to catch the vision.

Summary on Church Mobilisation

1 Biblical lifestyle of the church members must be in evidence.
2 Leader must be supportive and involved.
3 Quality and relevant training.
4 Regular support for volunteers.
5 Emphasis on developing relationships with PWAs and the community.
6 Include support for families.
7 It can take up to eighteen months for an effective programme to develop.
8 Clear liaison and communication with the local community.
9 More difficult to develop in urban areas.

The following biblical texts are drawn upon by TAIP. We can see their relevance for today, especially for those infected and affected by HIV/AIDS.

• Called to Care

2 Corinthians 1, verses 3 and 4: "Praise be to the God and Father of our Lord Jesus Christ, the Father of compassion

and the God of all comfort, who comforts us in all our troubles, so that we can comfort those in any trouble with the comfort we ourselves have received from God."

We have been given much by God and we have the responsibility to reach out to others in practical, caring compassion.

• The example of Jesus

Mark 1, verses 40 to 45. " A man with leprosy came to him (Jesus) and begged him on his knees, 'If you are willing you can make me clean.' Filled with compassion, Jesus reached out his hand and touched the man. 'I am willing' he said. 'Be clean!' Immediately the leprosy left him and he was cured."

We may not be able to touch and cure, but here we see that Jesus was filled with compassion for a person who in the times of the New Testament was not only afflicted by a disease, but suffered the prejudice and rejection of the community. Lepers were even seen as cursed, yet Jesus talked with this man and touched him.

• The call to be non-judgemental

John 8 verses 2 to 11. The woman caught in adultery, and the judgemental attitude of the religious leaders of the day. verse 7 - " If anyone of you is without sin, let him be the first to throw a stone at her."

No one did, including Jesus who was without sin. Should we not follow this example and show compassion and not judgement or prejudice against people with HIV, whether they have innocently contracted the virus, or not?

• The call to serve practically and sacrificially

Luke 10 verses 25 to 37. The parable of the Good Samaritan.

Mercy was shown to a man, who was most probably a Jew, by a Samaritan, the Jew's enemy. Yet the Samaritan gave time, his donkey, his medicines and money to care for the injured man — he showed mercy; Jesus says to us "Go and do like wise" verse 37.

- ## The call to advocacy and care for the marginalised

Isaiah 1 verse 17 "Seek justice, rescue the oppressed, defend the orphan, plead for the widow" The language is strong, proactive and action based.

- ## The church has a message that offers the framework for life

HIV/AIDS prevention should be part of a wider teaching on lifeskills that equips individuals to develop themselves and to counter pressures, including those that lead to increased vulnerability to HIV infection. The Word of God offers the framework for life and for hope; the church is obligated to tell others. This includes assisting members of communities in developing safe behaviour that can prevent the spread of HIV.

The AIC (Africa Inland Church) Kenya AIDS Team has developed, to great benefit, materials that utilise the bible for guidance in HIV/AIDS prevention, sex education and relationship development. Utilising materials from other parts of Africa and so "not reinventing the wheel" they have worked not only with local churches, but in their associated schools and importantly in Theological colleges, where the church leaders of tomorrow are equipped with Bible based skills and resources.

- ## A people of prayer

Ephesians 3 verses 14 - 21 includes a verse where Paul prays "that out of his [God's] glorious riches he may strengthen you with power through his Spirit in your inner being". Prayer for people infected and affected is essential. And prayer support for those involved in the work is also essential. This work is draining, physically, emotionally and spiritually, God's help is needed at every step of the way.

Community based response to HIV/AIDS Case Study — Chikankata Hospital Zambia

With the advent of the HIV/AIDS epidemic in southern Zambia, the response of Chikankata Hospital (Salvation Army) was to develop designated AIDS wards and comprehensive community and prevention services. However, it soon became apparent that there were too many people for the in-patient services to handle, and that many of the needs should and could be met by care services based in the community. Therefore, in1987 a Home Based Care (HBC) programme linked to hospital diagnosis, counselling, education and treatment was established.

This programme allowed people to be cared for in their own homes, and created opportunities to train families in the care of people living with HIV/AIDS (PWAs) and discuss HIV/AIDS education and prevention with families and the wider community. The HBC teams are multidisciplinary and include community nurses, nutritionists, and counsellors.

The HBC programme at Chikankata soon developed into a comprehensive HIV/AIDS programme including: in-hospital counselling AIDS education schools, child support programmes and technical assistance programmes for other organisations. Chikankata has developed a diverse but integrated approach to supporting the local community in combating HIV/AIDS. The programmes that are developed are tailored to meet the needs of different sections of the community.

Local communities in co-operation with Chikankata hospital have developed successful programmes providing care for persons with HIV infection.

These community-based programmes belong to the community that benefits from the services, not to the aspirations of an NGO or health care institution. The community is not necessarily restricted to a geographical area, but rather the term 'community-based' denotes that the local community owns it. The result of the link between home care, prevention and general community development has been an investment in a community not so readily achieved through hospital inpatient care. Furthermore, home care proved to be 50% cheaper than inpatient care. But to obtain such savings requires good planning and management. Community based care still has many costs attached, including the training and support of volunteers.

Holistic care, whereby the physical, social, spiritual, economic and psychological needs of both the individual and the community are met, is of paramount importance to the team at Chikankata. Such diverse needs can only be met by working with all those that contribute to a community, that is, individuals, families, communities, government institutions and the NGOs working together.

However, the expectations of many in the communities in the Chikankata area were increasingly that the Hospital, and not themselves, would meet many of their needs. And not only those related to HIV/AIDS, but often those related to other aspects of their lives, such as income generation, food production and schools.

The management of the hospital recognised that the use of paid hospital–based community care teams was expensive and that they were increasingly unable to meet the growing workload as HIV prevalence increased. One manager said the community health care structure was being used as a 'Neighbourhood Watch Scheme' that the community used, to ask for help on a wide range of community issues.

The response of the hospital management was to meet with the local leaders and communities and share their concerns that they could not continue to meet all the demands being made upon them. The result was the development of Care and Prevention Teams (CPTs) which are run by the community and not the hospital.

Care and Prevention teams have the following components:

- Community elects the CPT committee members
- The CPT address not only health issues but general development matters.
- Local key stakeholders are invited to join the committee e.g. Volunteer Health Workers, business men and women.
- The local church is not forced to join, and is encouraged to take on a servant role, rather than leadership role based on prescriptive authority. To be a servant is to be lower than the one we serve, to show the sacrificial love of Christ.
- Hospital-based staff work as team members.

The CPT works with their communities to highlight and rank them according to their perceived importance. This is followed by an identification of available resources: environmental (water, roads, trees, fertile land), services (hospitals, clinics, donors, banks, schools, NGOs) and human resources (teachers, farmers, politicians, committed individuals). A shortage of money does not mean a shortage of other resources.

- The CPT and community agree on a management structure and plan of action to provide most of the resources and activities required to respond to the community.
- An influential individual from the local community, or someone particularly committed, is selected by the community to act as the main motivator and link person.
- The CPT then negotiates with the hospital staff to agree the assistance that can be offered by the hospital to support the community's efforts. This could include regular monitoring and evaluation.
- Above all, the CPT strategy encourages the community to take on responsibility for the provision of caring for fellow members of the community who are chronically ill (not only those ill due to HIV/AIDS). Furthermore, care is not restricted to those who are ill, but also those affected by the illness, that is, of dependants, most often children and elderly parents.
- The CPT is not only concerned with the provision of HIV/AIDS care, but also the prevention of HIV/AIDS. And their focus is on behaviour change. As care of individuals is provided, opportunities for raising awareness and then addressing the underlying issue of behaviour change in the lives of individuals and communities (see below).

To quote Dapheton Siame a member of the Chikankata management team:

"This is not a new way of working, but finding again our old ways of [community] working". Dapheton and the other members of the Chikankata team are fully committed to providing a Christian response to communities affected by AIDS, the unconditional care of Christ. And this, Christ-like attitude of unconditional care, has seen them serving the community and working in full co-operation with communities, so that, together they combat AIDS.

Why HIV/AIDS is a major development issue

HIV/AIDS contributes to poverty and is a product of poverty. It strikes predominantly the sexually active, who are most often the economically active, the subsistence farmers, factory workers, urban professionals or mothers and carers of the elderly.

HIV/AIDS therefore impacts all aspects of development from education and women's rights to economic development programmes. So there is a need for HIV/AIDS programmes to research and act on the context within which they work. Likewise other development programmes must not ignore HIV/AIDS and the devastating undermining impact it can have on their projects. What is called for is an integrated approach.

Integrated Approach to HIV/AIDS

For example those training traditional birth attendants or irrigation workers can highlight the need for them to address the issue of HIV/AIDS. There is also the need for HIV/AIDS programmes to be internally integrated, to approach the issue holistically in the case of each person helped. Providing practical care alone only meets physical needs of people. There are also very real emotional needs as people face prejudice and rejection, and spiritual needs as they are facing death. Care must therefore encompass counselling by appropriately trained and supported workers.

Consult with, listen and act on the needs of people living with AIDS. It is they who are most in need and who can give critical insights to a programmes work. They need to be fully integrated into the programme development.

Holistic care, whereby the physical, social, spiritual, economic and psychological needs of both the individual and the community are met is of paramount importance to the most effective of AIDS programmes. Such diverse needs can only be met by all those affected individuals, families, communities, government institutions and other NGOs working together in an integrated way.

Advocacy

Advocacy is often a new activity for Churches and Christian AIDS NGOs (non-government organisations), many of which have previously felt it best to avoid the political arena and to concentrate on care and prevention.

However many Churches and NGOs are increasingly finding that they must act as advocates for PWAs and communities affected by AIDS. There are issues of justice with an absence of others to speak on their behalf. Many churches and Christian NGOs are acting as advocates for PWAs when they seek improved health care from clinics. But this has not necessarily led to planned strategies of how to respond to other advocacy needs.

Issues for advocates

- Develop relationships with key people and organisations.
- Try not to speak on behalf of PWAs and communities unless they agree.
- Facilitate meetings between marginalised groups and people of power.
- Be aware that prejudices and fears are often strong and will take time to change.
- Advocacy happens at many levels, local and national. From advocacy in a local clinic to national church leaders creating the right national environment for advocacy by others at more local levels.

Orphans Case Study — Bethany Trust, Zimbabwe

One of the most heartbreaking and also striking social consequences of the AIDS epidemic is the number of orphans and in many cases the increase of child-headed households. The responsibility for income and care, sometimes not only for siblings but also for their ailing parents and elderly grandparents, is falling increasingly on the shoulders of children.

When assisting orphans, it is not practical and rarely is it appropriate to restrict help to those who have lost parents due to AIDS. Be as inclusive as you are able to those orphaned from other causes, indeed to any children in need, irrespective of whether they are orphans or not. Very often children will be supporting parents who are ill and acting as their carers. To offer school fees only to those children affected by HIV/AIDS risks creating an imbalance in the community and increasing stigmatisation and prejudice.

It is also important that programmes to support orphans always look to the longer term future: are they going to be able to support themselves as they grow up? Are communities going to be able to develop their own capacity to help in a sustainable way, without external funding?

The principle of empowering the local community to care for their orphans has been central to the work of The Bethany Trust in Zimbabwe. Founded by Susie Howe, an HIV nurse specialist of several years, she found herself in Zimbabwe and felt compelled to work with local Christians to provide sustainable care for orphans in their communities. Local churches and Christians are encouraged and trained to equip communities to care for the increasing numbers of children in need.

Bethany will begin by discussing with communities and their orphans their needs, concerns and what possible solutions the community can identify for the challenges ahead of them. Volunteers are then trained to provide emotional and practical support for orphans. This could include guidance on planting crops to guidance on growing up. They speak to children, listen to them and then speak up for them when required.

But this work is not restricted to child-headed households, but also to assisting any family that has suffered the loss of a parent. This is particularly critical for supporting the increasing number of grandparents who now act as sole carers for their grandchildren.

By enabling families and communities to care for orphans and not sending them off to orphanages where they may become stigmatised (especially if it has 'AIDS Orphanage' written over the door) the children gain so much. They maintain their sense of belonging to a family and a community. This has often proven to benefit children emotionally, but also practically as they are supported in the present and learn relevant skills to survive long term in their home areas.

[A similar methodology has also been repeated in Chikankata. The hospital is now moving away from providing school fees for individual orphans towards supporting the economic development of local communities and when grants are made they are for schools, not just individuals. These new initiatives are entitled not AIDS specific, but CHIN, Children in Need. This is a response headed by the local communities, that seeks to assist all children in need, not only orphans. It is an integrated approach that mobilises communities and strengthens bonds between children and their community. This reduces the stigmatisation of orphans and in particular, orphans who have lost their parents due to HIV/AIDS.]

In the past people have often built orphanages as a response to the needs of orphans. But the Bethany Project has encouraged and trained communities to such an effective extent that in five years it has mobilised the care of over 6,000 orphans in the district of Zvishavane alone. Orphanages can be seen as the last safety net, but before that point is reached there is the existing family and community structures to be drawn upon.

However every situation is different and in some communities other ways to support orphans have been successfully developed in locally sensitive and appropriate ways.

Summary on responding to Orphans

- Involve orphans, listen to them.
- Empower families and communities.
- Support to all families in need, not only those affected by HIV/AIDS.
- Aim wherever possible to keep children in their communities.
- Provide skills that will sustain families e.g. farming and income generation activities.

Refugees

HIV/AIDS has been seen to spread more easily in times of instability when social practices that often protect individuals are disrupted or even broken down completely. This includes protective sexual practices. In early 2002 there were an estimated 15 million refugees in the world. Three-quarters of them in Africa and 80% were women and children. In addition there were an unknown number of displaced people who had been forced from their homes but had not crossed country borders.

HIV can spread at times of social crisis and its impact is greatest in developing countries, the very countries least equipped to combat the crises.

In emergency situations of mass movement, HIV often seems less important than food, shelter, water, emergency health care and security. But what are the long-term effects of not prioritising the risks of HIV transmission? Relief workers must ask the question: are displaced people at greater risk of HIV infection and should this need not also be met at the same time as the short-term issues of security, shelter and nourishment?

Poverty alleviation and Income generation activities

Where there is poverty AIDS seems to follow close behind. And the evidence is that AIDS thrives in areas of poverty. The red light district of Mumbai, India is full of HIV + girls whose poverty stricken families have sold them to the owners of brothels. Income Generation Activities (IGAs) can be an effective intervention for the support of individuals, families, programmes and institutions, but they must be done with care and skill, particularly in the context of HIV/AIDS.

It is important to consider the abilities of PWAs in relation to their health status. It must be remembered that an individual may not always be able to work on IGAs due to poor health, and that it may be necessary to supplement IGAs with welfare grants. Furthermore, IGAs that involve the families and supporting communities of PWAs will assist in the sustainability of IGAs during periods when people are too ill to play a full part in an activity.

The integration of people who are not HIV positive, or whose HIV status is not known into an economic activity may also be an opportunity to increase the acceptance and integration within the local community of PWAs.

Issues for Income Generation Activities

- Previous experience of IGA management is essential.
- The skills required are very specific and critical to avoid wasting money and causing disappointment
- The activity must be viable, there must be a market and skills available. Seek proven expert help to test these issues.
- Activities have often centred on women, which can lead to increased burden on them rather than self-reliance. As with any programme every step of the planning and implementation must be thought through. Again an external advisor with relevant experience can help.

The Need for Good Management

For work of any kind to be effective, there is a fundamental need for good management. Without good management a community's needs will not be heard and motivated volunteers or the skills of professionals will be wasted.

Management includes many elements but two possible sub divisions are; leadership and organising.

Organisation

Information is important at each stage of the programme. To begin with research and evaluation of the needs of the community in which you wish to operate will give the basic information to form a plan and develop an organisational structure. The continued gathering of information will allow monitoring and the development of the work

Research issues

1   What does the community say is needed?
2   What do those with AIDS want?
3   What evidence is there for this?
4   What resources are available in the community?

Are other resources required, how are they to be obtained?

5   Does the church/organisation want to meet the needs identified, do they sit well within the ethos of the organisation?

6   Does the organisation have the capacity in terms of personnel, structure and resources to work with the community in combating HIV/AIDS and other development issues?

7   Are there other organisations that are already doing all or part of the work. If so, why set up another organisation, will this not be wasting precious resources? Or can you work in co-operation for increased effectiveness?

8   Visit other projects, utilise proven methods and materials. Why reinvent the wheel?

Planning

1   Having identified answers to the above it is important to set objectives with key indicators i.e. measurements to monitor progress. Use SMART objectives: Specific, Measurable, Achievable, Relevant, Time-bound.

2   Again those affected, community, staff and volunteers should be involved.

Monitoring

1   Information should be gathered and reviewed on a regular basis to monitor success or failure to meet the goals.

2   Failure to meet certain goals does not mean that the programme is not succeeding but could mean some goals need to be altered. This should take place in full consultation with staff, volunteers and the community. What is important is the effectiveness of the work, not out of date goals.

3   Review meetings should also be held with those who receive the service, the community and also with others working in the area.

Organisational structure

1   An organisational structure should be prepared and made known to all in the organisation. People benefit from knowing who they are responsible to.
2   If volunteers are to be used ensure they are motivated.
3   Employed staff should have relevant experience and skills.
4   Relevant initial training is critical and should be followed by regular updates.
5   All staff, paid and volunteers should have a support structure and receive regular appraisals, with opportunity to comment and input to the development of the organisation.
6   Clear and open financial management.

Leadership

Qualities in leadership

As stated above the most effective NGO responses to HIV/AIDS have been by those organisations that have not only sought to co-operate with the community, but have sought to serve. This serving of others should be central to leadership. A leader who is humble and models service will more likely produce a team and organizsation that serves others.

1   When leaders and managers are being selected it is good to look for proven leadership and management experience: have they been effective in mobilising others to achieve something effective?

2   A leader should focus on developing quality relationships. Relationships within and outside of the organisation, with community leaders, PWAs, other organisations. Good relationships with staff can be the basis for the development of an effective team, of learning of new opportunities and of learning about frustrations and barriers to effectiveness. Ultimately the leader and the organisation are dependent on the whole team.

3   Good relationships will allow a leader to influence for the good and reduce the need for over directing of staff.

4   Instead a leader will be facilitating the skills and motivation of people to be utilised effectively.

5   There is a need for vision from a leader, vision that is clear and understandable by others.

6   The leader should have empathy with people. The ability to put themselves "in the shoes" of the people they lead.

7   An ability to understand (listen and reflect) and be understood (communicate well).

8   A manager leader will require accountability from their staff and they too must be accountable to a governance board or committee.

Ultimately in all Christian leadership there should be the visible qualities of being Christ-centred, biblical thinking, humility, integrity and servanthood. These qualities are more important than any technical skill or specific experience in HIV/AIDS work. Such people can help facilitate communities and individuals respond to HIV/AIDS.

Time for Action

Lists like the ones above can make people feel that they are not qualified or they have nothing they can do themselves.

The MOST important thing of all is to DO SOMETHING. As said before, it costs nothing to care, and you need no organising to go and visit a neighbour in need, or to talk to your own relatives about the risks of HIV, or indeed to lend someone this book, or to get involved in an existing programme.

The battle against AIDS will not be won by great programmes. It will be won as millions of ordinary men and women in every nation rise up as a people movement, determined to take AIDS seriously and to make a real difference. And as those who belong to Christ, we have a message of strength and hope as well as of health and wholeness.

You can't change the whole world but today you can change someone's world somewhere.

"For a list of useful organisations and web links as well as other resources, please look at the ACET International Alliance website: http://www.acet-international.org"

ACET International Alliance

The ACET International Alliance is a growing community of independent AIDS programmes in many parts of the world, that originally began in UK under the ACET name in 1988. ACET stands for AIDS, Care, Education and Training and was founded by Dr Patrick Dixon. Alliance members are united in a common aim to see an effective Christian response to AIDS:

- Unconditional, compassionate care for all affected by HIV / AIDS
- Life-saving prevention respecting and upholding the historic teachings of the church
- Effective training with a holistic approach to personal and community development

The Alliance consists of

- National Resource Centres: centres of excellence that are actively seeking to be an encouragement and resource to others in different parts of the world who share the same values and vision
- Partner Programmes: organisations providing HIV-related services
- Development Partners: international organisations which act as resources to different parts of the Alliance

The Alliance is a network of organisations co-operating together, rather than a funding organisation, does not have a big central administration and does not make central grants.

The main work of the Alliance is carried out by the National Resource Centres, programmes based in countries such as England, Scotland, Ireland, India, Uganda, Thailand, the Czech Republic and Slovakia.

New Programme Partners join the Alliance on the recommendation of an existing National Resource Centre, after a period of working together. Members commit themselves to effective Christian action in the AIDS field, and to sharing / networking expertise, experience and resources as they are able.

Further information about ACET International Partners near you and what the Alliance does, as well as latest news about HIV, action packs and many other useful materials is all available on the website:

http://www.acet-international.org

e-mail: isdixon@dircon.co.uk

Further copies of this book may be ordered free for distribution in the poorest nations in the following languages: English, Russian, Spanish, French, Hungarian, Czech, Romanian, Turkish, Urdu and Paite.

Operation Mobilisation

Operation Mobilisation is pleased to co-publish and sponsor this edition, and is totally committed to seeing churches everywhere make a compassionate, caring and practical response to all those affected by HIV and AIDS, as well as helping to save lives.

OM was founded by George Verwer, whose energy, originality and challenge to discipleship and World evangelism touched many people. Emphasis on 'Training through doing' was a central feature of the many teams that went out, in different parts of the World. The vision and eventual purchase of OM's mercy ships probably put OM on the map more than any other single factor.

Today, OM is a dynamic, global ministry with almost 3000 full-time staff working in over 80 countries. It is committed to working in partnership with churches and other Christian organisations for the the purpose of world mission. The different ministries of OM provide speakers for churches, conferences and seminars, experienced training in all forms of evangelism, leadership and pastoral care and a wealth of resources, including videos, books, presentation materials and prayer cards.

http://www.om.org
http://www.ombooks.org

WHO AIDS Treatment Programme

After long delays and political fights, the wealthiest nations have woken up to the fact that the majority affected cannot afford antiretroviral treatment, even though it prolongs life of most with HIV, and can prevent up to 66% of all infections in babies born to infected mothers. A new initiative aims to get free antiviral tablets, to at least 3 million people in developing countries. This will also encourage people to be tested, because there is treatment available. Testing is a powerful way to prevent spread: those who are negative are motivated to stay that way, and those who are positive are more likely to change behaviour if they know they could infect someone else.

This is the system (still being developed at time of writing):

- WHO provides Department of Health in the country with medicines
- Organisations apply in-country to partner with WHO and the government
- Supply is given (probably in boxes containing enough for one person for one month)
- Other resources are provided eg instant testing equipment, together with training of a nurse or nurses (no doctor is needed)
- Local population is encouraged by organisation to be tested, after counselling
- Those who are positive, and have clearly defined patterns of ill health, or are pregnant, are started on treatment after a

simple blood test, repeated every two weeks
- Therapy is usually taken for the rest of the person's life unless stopped to allow the blood test to return to more normal levels
- Careful records are kept of how the drug supplies have been used
- Records are shown to the distribution centre, to get further supplies

Smaller organisations and churches will need to partner with larger groups to get access. WHO will be monitoring each country to ensure good flow of medicine to organisations, and welcomes information about problems on the ground in making this work. See http://www.who.org

Christian AIDS/HIV National Alliance — (CANA)

CANA was set up in 1998, based in New Delhi, as an Indian national network of Christian practitioners responding to HIV/AIDS. It is formed by various like-minded individuals, multisectoral development organizations and institutions across the country. It acts as a coalition organization that facilitates a concerted effort among its organizations/members by building their response mechanism in tackling the complex issues in dealing with HIV/AIDS. CANA endeavours to make an effective and positive contribution in minimising and preventing the suffering caused by the HIV virus in the life of individuals, families, communities and society as a whole. CANA plays a vital role in developing responses through strategic interventions in terms of:

- **Communication & Advocacy:** Promote good and Christian practice through exposure, training and communication materials
- **Networking:** Mobilise national and regional Christian HIV/AIDS networks to become an effective resource for a Christian response through involvement and sharing of expertise and resources.
- **Action Research & Capacity Building:** Help train church and related organizations in technical, spiritual, social, psychological and management issues.

CANA is not a direct project-implementing agency. That is the focus of a large number of the constituent partners of the CANA network. CANA is a facilitating role — nationwide.

Join the Coalition!

In terms of the future, a great challenge lies ahead and we need to develop integrated and holistic approaches for the vulnerable as well as those marginalized because of HIV/AIDS. We call upon the people of God to respond with the love of Christ in non-judgemental and practical ways. Our God expects us to be carers, healers and advocates to restore people and lives. There is an immediate need for a Christian intervention in prevention, care, justice and development. We encourage you to become a CANA network member and work together in co-operation to face the challenges before us by offering healing, wholeness and hope to the millions of persons, families and communities suffering caused by HIV/AIDS in India.

Further copies of this edition of *AIDS and YOU* can be ordered from CANA for distribution in India. For other nations and language editions, contact ACET International Alliance.

For More information contact:
cana@vsnl.com
www.cana-india.org
or
Emmanuel Hospital Association
808/92, Nehru Place, New Delhi - 110 019, India
Phone: 91-011-30882018, 30882009, Fax: 30882019
Email: centraloffice@eha-health.org

General Inquiries:
Email: info@eha-health.org
Website: www.eha-health.org